Holy Silence
The Gift of Quaker Spirituality

This book belongs to:

Sr   Ann

Catherine

Holy Silence
The Gift of Quaker Spirituality

J. BRENT BILL

PARACLETE PRESS
BREWSTER, MASSACHUSETTS

2006 Third Printing
2005 First and Second Printing

Copyright © 2005 by J. Brent Bill
ISBN 1-55725-420-6

Library of Congress Cataloging-in-Publication Data
Bill, J. Brent, 1951-
Holy silence: the gift of Quaker spirituality / J. Brent Bill.
   p. cm.
Includes bibliographical references.
ISBN 1-55725-420-6
1. Silence—Religious aspects—Society of Friends. 2. Society of Friends—Doctrines. I. Title.
   BX7748.S5B55 2005
   248'.088 2896—dc22   2004028952

10   9   8   7   6   5   4   3

Published by Paraclete Press
Brewster, Massachusetts
www.paracletepress.com
Printed in the United States of America

"Never marry but for love;
but see that thou lovest what is lovely."
—*William Penn*

For Lovely Nancy

CONTENTS

Author's Note
ABOUT THE QUIETUDE QUERIES

Throughout chapters two through five you will find "Quietude Queries." These queries are intended to provide a "time-out" for reflection. *Queries* is the Friends practice of examining our souls and seeking clarity. These questions and exercises help to give time to seek truth about ourselves and our spiritual condition, and to tap into Divine insight. Queries guide us in listening for God's voice in our lives. They are not intended to provide mystical experiences of God, though that may occur.

Quietude means a state of peace and quiet.

These exercises are provided to guide you in peacefully listening to God's voice and to your own soul in silence. As you read the Quietude Queries, let your mind and soul fill with words, ideas, or images. In silence God gently invites us into the Holy.

CHAPTER ONE

Silence
The Quaker Sacrament

My short, red-headed wife, Nancy, and I marveled as fall colors moved down the mountain across from the Vermont country inn where we were staying. For seven days we watched the golds, russets, and oranges merge into the greens of the valleys. We stood on top of mountains with views of several states and of Canada while the wind whipped what little hair I have left. We wound our rental car along closed-in, curvy, country roads bordered by rushing streams and waterfalls, never able to see more than a few hundred yards ahead of us or a few hundred feet up. For two flatlanders from Indiana, the scenery put us close to sensory overload. I was almost ready to fly back to the safety of Indiana's landscape with its gentler risings and fallings and bigger sky.

But it was Sunday morning. *First Day* morning, as older Quakers say. So, before heading to the airport, we drove to South Starksboro *Friends* Meeting. It was a setting dreamed up by the Vermont tourism council—an 1826 era plain, white, clapboard meetinghouse, its rectangular, steeple-lessness tucked into a clearing halfway up a mountainside. Tombstones dotted the meetinghouse grounds. Sunlight threw the carvings into stark relief.

We took our obligatory leaf peeper pictures while Vermonters indulgently smiled on. Then we made our way across the grass, through the front door, over the wood floor, and settled onto the benches. No modern, padded, or comfortable church pews for us simple Friends. No central heating, either. A black wood stove clanked, stoked for Sunday *Meeting*. Afghans and comforters sat stacked on one of the benches for those wanting to ward off the chill. Sunlight softened by old, clear, wavy glassed windows filled the room. As did God's glory.

It was a traditional Friends service conducted in silence. This small group numbered less than a tenth of the Quaker congregation we normally worship with in Indiana. There was no bulletin, no paid preacher, no choir. There was an old pump organ, but it sat tucked in a corner and needed dusting. Any music or message would arise out of the silence—but only if God's Spirit led someone to sing or share. The preacher in me looked for a clock—it always hangs where the parson, if not the congregation, can see it. There wasn't one. In spite of that, we all fell silent at about the same time. Some of us bowed our heads. Others wiggled in the benches for a moment, searching perhaps for a comfortable hollow worn by someone's backside. Exterior sound fell away, save for the ticking of the warming wood stove, the popping of burning wood, and the occasional stifled cough.

I looked and saw Nancy, backlit by sunlight through the window. She sat with head bowed, blue eyes open, and hands folded in her lap. My gaze returned to the wood-planked floor between my feet. I took off my glasses and closed my eyes. Soon interior noise fell away. Thoughts of the late-afternoon flight to Indianapolis, worries about work waiting for me at the office, and the flood of minutiae that swamps my mind when outside noise stops, slowly vanished—dropping into a well of holy silence. I let myself be guided into the deep waters of the soul.

That is when it happened. The only thing I can compare it to is the Catholic belief that in the "celebration of Mass . . . Christ is really present through Holy Communion to the assembly gathered in His name." It is the same way with silence for Quakers. Friends believe that Christ is actually present—except we have no host to elevate or priest to preside. Rather, we believe that when our hearts, minds, and souls are still, and we wait expectantly in holy silence, that the presence of Christ comes among us. That October day, on the side of the Green Mountains, Jesus was good to His word that, "where two or three come together in my name, there am I with them." In the silence, where outer and inner noise ceased, we became what

Quakers call *a gathered meeting*–gathered together and with Jesus. We sensed Him in the electrified air. I felt charged with an awareness of the miraculous–the marrow of my bones hummed in holy recognition of the One who had stood at the dawn of creation and called the world into being. And it did not just happen to me.

The presence of Christ among us changed the hour. Instead of enduring sixty minutes of dragging, stagnant silence, we felt that the first chapter of John's Gospel had come to life in Vermont–"The Word became flesh and made his dwelling among us. We have seen his glory, the glory of the One and Only, who came from the Father, full of grace and truth." As if something had been lit deep inside and now shone from their faces, we saw "grace and truth" reflected in the people around us. It was a true Sabbath–free from noise and busyness as we worshiped and were spiritually fed. Though no outward words were spoken, no formal prayers recited, no music played softly in the background to set a mood, God had worked His way into the deepest parts of our hearts and out to our fingers and toes and noses.

Then, too soon, Meeting ended. Don, the person next to me, shifted and shook my hand–a sign among Friends that *Meeting for Worship* is over. No loud amen's or formal benedictions for us. Instead we smiled. For a long while no one said anything. No one wanted to break the holy moment. But then our humanness broke in. Small talk broke out. Friends asked for news of mutual acquaintances back in Indiana. Huddled by the wood

[handwritten margin note: ← Result of Silence]

box, three men discussed who should close off the woodstove. Still, even in this after Meeting chitchat, we sensed that we were now part of each other and of God in a way we had not felt just an hour earlier.

Nancy and I had come to Vermont hoping for some respite from eldercare and work. We were leaving with spirits rejuvenated from an experience that had nothing to do with fall foliage. The Creator had breathed a blessing upon us.

Even as I tell you that story, I am struck by the absurdity of trying to write about silence. Who needs words about silence? Why not just keep silent? Besides, how do you put into words something that is unlike words?

The only justification for trying is that the Friends' approach to silence is a pathway to God that sates my spirit unlike anything else I have ever experienced. Yes, I appreciate liturgy, hymn singing, sermons, and other religious rituals. But Quaker silence speaks to the spiritual condition in a way nothing else does. This Quaker silence is not just for me or old men on oat boxes or in classic movies, either. It offers a profound spiritual encounter for any woman or man hungry for a fresh way of connecting with God.

Friendly silence speaks—yes, *speaks*, oddly enough—to the hunger for silence that we see in people all around us. Look at the rising interest in silent retreats and contemplative reading. Something in our souls tells us that getting quiet is a good way to meet God, no matter whether our souls are anxious or settled, swamped by insecurity or swathed in peace.

The prophet Elijah found that out shortly after his showdown with the prophets of Baal on Mount Carmel. Elijah triumphed, and the idolaters lost—their lives. Then Queen Jezebel sent an un-thank you note to Elijah saying, "You killed my prophets. I'll kill you." Elijah's spiritual zeal evaporated, and he got out of town, praying as he went, "God, I've had enough. Take my life." God did not oblige. Instead God told him:

> "Go out and stand on the mountain before the LORD, for the LORD is about to pass by." Now there was a great wind, so strong that it was splitting mountains and breaking rocks in pieces before the LORD, but the LORD was not in the wind; and after the wind an earthquake, but the LORD was not in the earthquake; and after the earthquake a fire, but the LORD was not in the fire; and after the fire a sound of sheer silence. When Elijah heard it, he wrapped his face in his mantle and went out and stood at the entrance of the cave.

Maybe that makes Elijah the first Friend. He learned that God was in "sheer silence." Other versions say "a still small voice" or a gentle "whisper." And what he heard in that sheer silence gave him hope and strength to go on living. What Elijah's story teaches us lies at the heart of Friends silence. This holy hush is about meeting

Jesus in an intimate way. Quaker silence encourages us to relax into the love of God until we hear the Spirit's voice whispering softly in our soul's ear.

When we really want to hear, and be heard by, someone we love, we do not go rushing into noisy crowds. Silence is a form of intimacy. That's how we experience it with our friends and lovers. As relationships grow deeper and more intimate, we spend more and more quiet time alone with our lover. We talk in low tones about the things that matter. We do not shout them to each other. We may shout about them to others, but quietness is the hallmark of love.

That is why Christ comes to us when our hearts and minds are silent and still. Quaker silence is pregnant with holy expectation. It is filled with anticipation that Jesus will be there. And not in some abstract, vaguely spiritual feel-good way, either. We believe that Christ comes in a physically present way in the same way that Catholics believe that when the host is elevated it becomes the literal body and blood of Jesus. It is not just some symbol. As Flannery O'Connor, the great Catholic writer, once said of Eucharist, "Well, if it's a symbol, to hell with it. . . . It is the center of existence for me; all the rest of life is expendable."

Friends feel that way about silence. The deep silence of the soul is our Eucharist. Rufus Jones, a Quaker mystic and writer of the twentieth century, said of sacramental silence, "it may be an intensified pause, a vitalized hush, a creative quiet, an actual moment of mutual and reciprocal correspondence with God. The actual meeting of man with God and God with man is the very crown and culmination of what we can do with our human life here on earth."

This actual meeting of us with God and God with us, as Jones defined it, makes Quaker silence different from other silences. Even other spiritual silences. But this meeting may not seem so different to an outsider who sees us practicing it. She would not see any angels descending. He would not notice halos appearing over our heads. There is no physical evidence of the life-changing activity going on inside us as we experience the love of God filling our souls. "Outwardly," says Friend Thomas Kelly, "all silences seem alike, as all minutes are alike by the clock. But inwardly the Divine Leader of worship directs us . . . and may in the silence bring an inward climax which is as definite as the climax of the Mass when the host is elevated in adoration."

This sacramental language may seem strong from a group that discarded rituals. But Quakers only abandoned rituals in favor of what they considered inner sacraments full of spiritual power. They found that they came to God and God came to them in holy silence. They feasted on Jesus in their hearts. Then they found power to live lives of faithful practice. Friends used silence to throw off the outward and move to the inward, mystical union with the Divine.

The psalmist urges us to "Be still, and know that I am God." Friends believe that this inward, mystical union is more likely to happen if we approach silence expectantly.

Even though the old Quaker joke calls us to, "Don't just do something, sit there," holy silence is more than just sitting there. If it isn't something more, then we'll become like the Quakers described by some English fishermen—"They Quakers just came here and sat and sat and nobody never said nothing, until at last they all died and so they gave it up."

Silence is something we do, not something done to us. It is a participatory act. It engages our heart, mind, soul, and body in listening for the voice of the Beloved. Quaker silence is not passive. After all, how could Holy Communion, which deepens our faith and fills us with passionate love for God, ever be inactive?

Silence allows us to actively pursue a new experience of God. It is open to all, not just Quakers. No one has a corner on living in silence with God. Active holy silence can be for you, as it is for Friends, a "Eucharist and Communion."

CHAPTER TWO

Turned Outside In
Spiritual Silence for Saints
and the Rest of Us

Root beer, the first American flag, fine milk
chocolates—all are Quaker inventions of
which we humble Friends are humbly proud.
If you don't believe me, check the backgrounds of
Charles Hires, Betsy Ross, and the Cadbury clan.
Quaker through and through. Sometimes Friends act
as if we invented holy silence, too. That's because it is
such an integral part of Quaker life. While we did
bring a certain refinement and slant to spiritual
silence, we have to admit that using silence as a spiritual
practice has a history almost as long as humankind's
spiritual seeking.

If we open some of humanity's oldest writing we
find that worshipers of Mithra, the Iranian god of light

and friendship, practiced silence. That's because they saw silence as a symbol for God. At the same time, in pre-Christian North America, Native Americans used silence as a spiritual discipline. Ohiyesa (which means *Winner*) was an eastern, woodland Sioux also known as Charles A. Eastman. He wrote, "Each soul must meet the morning sun, the new sweet earth, and the Great Silence alone! What is Silence? It is the Great Mystery! The Holy Silence is His voice!"

The faiths born in the East—Hinduism, Buddhism, and Taoism—have long cultivated an appreciation for silence. They believe silence is essential to spiritual life. They see silence as a mark of spiritual maturity. The Chinese scripture called the *Tao Te Ching* says, "Those who know do not talk. Those who talk do not know." Those revered as the holiest people in the East—gurus, bhikkhus, and Zen Masters—are people of few words. They speak little because they believe, as Gandhi said, that "In the attitude of silence the soul finds the path in a clearer light, and what is elusive and deceptive resolves itself into crystal clearness." That's why Zen and other Eastern meditations are best practiced in total silence.

In Eastern religions silence is a prerequisite to spiritual purification and growth. Eastern religions teach that silence leads to inner awareness, wisdom, compassion, and loving kindness. Hindus and Buddhists believe silence is a way of achieving Moksha (freedom or salvation), nirvana (right-mindedness), or Buddhahood. In Theravada, silence helps a person to finally realize the ultimate goal—clarity of wisdom.

In the Judeo-Christian tradition, the Old Testament abounds with examples of silence as a means of meeting God. The most famous is the earlier-mentioned exhortation to "Be still and know that I am God."

The Hebrew Scriptures also show that silence is a way to wisdom—"A wise man will keep quiet until just the right moment," for example. While the writer of Ecclesiasticus seems more concerned with silence as a way of gaining respect in the community, there is, nonetheless, recognition that silence—the absence of talking—leads us to wisdom. The Bible writers held that wisdom was one of God's attributes. Silence leads us to wisdom—and an imitation, limited by our human nature as it is, of God.

We also have the Old Testament example of Habakkuk standing at his guard post, keeping watch to see what God had to say. Habakkuk had some hard questions and complaints for God: Why are people suffering? Why is there violence in the land? Why won't You help? So Habakkuk stands at his post, silent, waiting to hear what God says. God answers Habakkuk. One thing that God says is that God "is in his holy temple; let all the earth keep silence before him." In so saying, God introduces the idea of silence as a way of worshiping.

Then there's Samuel. He heard a voice calling in the still of the night. The voice called until Samuel, at Eli's urging, accepted that it was the Lord calling. God called three times until Samuel stilled himself enough to listen—both outwardly, while lying on his bed, and inwardly in his heart. When he became quiet in holy awe, God and Samuel spoke heart to heart. Samuel's silence, as a young boy, and his attitude of listening showed his love for God. It also shows us that people of all ages—even the young, like Samuel—long for a deep spiritual connection with God. Samuel's response was simply, "Speak, Yahweh, for your servant is listening." Samuel believed God would speak. God did not disappoint him.

Quietude Query

🕊 Relax your body and mind.

🕊 Breathe deeply.

🕊 Put down the book.

🕊 Think about the following Quietude Query slowly and gently. Savor each thought.

🕊 Have I ever had questions I wanted to ask God? I'll think of one, take a long breath, and ask it out of silence.

In the New Testament we find many examples of Jesus' seeking the silence of solitude, even group solitude. He urged the same of His followers. After the murder of John the Baptist, the Gospel of Mark tells us that "The apostles returned to Jesus, and told him all that they had done and taught. And he said to them, 'Come away by yourselves to a lonely place, and rest a while.' For many were coming and going, and they had no leisure even to eat. And they went away in the boat to a lonely place by themselves." There's no record of anything being said on the boat trip to that "lonely" place. In light of the grief, bewilderment, and depression they were feeling, perhaps silence was the only thing that spoke to their condition.

We read in the book of Galatians about Paul's going to Arabia after his conversion, to be alone with God. Unlike a televangelist who gets a message and then springs into action via the airwaves, Paul moved away from action and into contemplation. He took time to reflect about what this encounter with the living Christ meant for his life and ministry before he began proclaiming his message.

The earliest Christian mystics, especially the desert fathers, used silence as an integral part of their religious discipline. In *Book the First, of the Sayings of the Holy Fathers*, Palladius reports:

> When Abba Arsenius was in the palace, he prayed to God and said, "O Lord, direct me how to live," and a voice came to him, saying, "Arsenius, flee from men, and thou shalt live." And when Arsenius was living the ascetic life in the monastery, he prayed to God the same prayer, and again he heard a voice saying unto

him, "Arsenius, flee, keep silence, and lead a
life of silent contemplation, for these are the
fundamental causes which prevent a man from
committing sin."

The desert fathers emphasized silence as more
than mere absence of sound. They saw it in a variety
of ways—flight from humankind, non-speech, quietude, solitude, silent prayer, and contemplation.
Their practice of silence varied according to their
own interpretations and needs. Organized sets of
rules about silence didn't appear until the monastic
orders arose, like the one established by Benedict of
Nursia in the late sixth century. Benedict's rule still
serves as the basic guide for Christians committed to
the monastic movement.

Despite such appreciation and formalization by the
Benedictines and a variety of saints, silence has not
always been seen as a way of reaching God—particularly
for folks not cloistered in convents and monasteries.
The medieval mystics were an exception. Many of them
managed to keep silent. One of the most famous of
them, Meister Eckhart, said in the fourteenth century:
"Nothing in all creation is so like God as silence." *The
Practice of Perfection and Christian Virtues*, written in 1609
by Alphonsus Rodriguez, a Spanish Jesuit, quotes a
number of saints, for example, St. Bernard of Clairvaux:
"Continual silence, and removal from the noise of the
things of this world and forgetfulness of them, lifts up
the heart and asks us to think of the things of heaven

and sets our heart upon them"; and St. Diodorus: silence is "the mother of holy and lofty thoughts."

Quietude Query

⤸ Relax your body and mind.

⤸ Breathe deeply.

⤸ Put down the book.

⤸ Think about the following Quietude Query slowly and gently. Savor each thought.

⤸ Why do I think Meister Eckhart said that "Nothing in all creation is so like God as silence"? Does silence fit my image of God?

Still, the Christianity-dominated West has had little appreciation for silence as spiritually useful. This is especially true in the time since the Reformation. This neglect of silence began in the sixteenth century with Martin Luther's emphasis on the "Word." Much of modern worship tends toward words, if not *the* Word. It moves away from silence. While many congregations have what they call a time of silent prayer, it often isn't silent. Many times an organ plays softly, or a worship leader gives "prayer suggestions." If there is true silence people start fidgeting. Let the silence go for more than a minute and people look to see if the worship leader has lost her place in the program. Even in the Catholic tradition, says my friend Sue, where there is quiet meditation following communion, depending on the parish and the priest, "this only lasts for ten seconds, or at the most for one and a half minutes."

In the United States today we find a blending of Eastern and Western religious practices in "Christian yoga." One example is Outstretched, Inc. This is a nonprofit outreach ministry of Jubilee Shores United Methodist Church in Fairhope, Alabama. Led by Susan Bordenkircher, this Christian approach uses yoga to calm minds and quiet souls "to the point that we can tune out the world's frequency and tune into God's frequency." Bordenkircher says that "Being quiet with God allows us to create enough psychological and spiritual space that God can truly create an inner sanctuary in us."

Far from advocating a syncretistic pastiche, Bordenkircher has attempted to introduce Christians to contemplative practice, all within the sanction of orthodox faith. The only sad part of this blending is that it looks outside Christianity for silence instead of embracing the rich tradition of Christian contemplation. It is as if silence and spirituality find validation only if they come from the East.

Also back in the U.S., but removed from any semblance of Christian practice, there are New Age silences like those espoused by Elizabeth Baron. Baron is a New Age "trance medium" who claims to channel St. Catherine of Siena. Baron says that, "As you learn the art of going into silence, you progress through mental, physical, and spiritual preparations toward the optimum meditative experience. You will take the steps to awareness as you get to know yourself on a deeper level, progressing through basic colour meditations, dream interpretation, and understanding the God in YOU."

There are also goddess silences, Wiccan silences, and other spiritual silences. All these, and the ones mentioned previously, show that Quaker Rufus Jones spoke to something universal when he wrote that silence is essential for "worship or as a method of preparing the soul for spiritual experiences." And while it may seem that all spiritual silences are alike—early Christian, Eastern, New Age—they aren't. Yes, they are all quiet. But, there are differences among them. There is something that sets Quaker silence apart from all the others. To see what that is we have to take a quick trip back in time.

Quietude Query

➣ Relax your body and mind.

➣ Breathe deeply.

➣ Put down the book.

➣ Think about the following Quietude Query slowly and gently. Savor each thought.

➣ What do I normally do to prepare my soul for a spiritual experience? Can I see silence as enhancing that?

Quakers sprang up in mid-seventeenth-century England. This was a time of great unrest in England, politically, socially, religiously. Huge armies surged back and forth across the countryside, fighting for control of the government, church, and the souls of men and women . . . well, mostly men. It was, as one Quaker historian put it, as if they were sort of Jehovah's Witnesses with guns. "Convert . . . or else."

Into this setting came the Seekers. These men and women—an important distinction—came from all the day's religious groups: Independents, Puritans, Anglicans, and Catholics. They worshiped in silence. They did so because they felt that they needed to be quiet and wait on God—not men—to speak. The Seekers were convinced that religious life consisted of deep inward spiritual experiences. So they rejected all outward sacraments, paid ministry, and church rites. They had no fight with rites. Rather they were disturbed at how rites and rituals had been co-opted by the state and by many clergy for political purposes. They saw holy silence as a way to encourage women and men on their spiritual journeys. It led them to a quiet inner place where God taught them that they "might come to receive freely from Him."

This hope of receiving freely from God led them to abandon religious rites and a paid clergy. "The less form in religion the better, since God is a Spirit; . . . the more silent, the more suitable to the language of a Spirit," wrote William Penn, one of the first converts. Penn urged all Christians to embrace silence as a religious practice, because he knew holy silence isn't about stillness, as such, but rather about encountering God in a living and vital holy hush. Still, these spiritually hungry, soulfully silent Seekers were largely directionless.

Along came George Fox. Fox was a young man whose whole life had been a spiritual quest. He agreed with Puritans that sin caused a gulf between God and humankind and that this divide could only be crossed if God reached toward us. So he went in search of a place where God made that reach. He visited "priests" and "professors" (those professing Christian faith) for advice. He found the quality of their advice lacking. It varied from "smoke tobacco" to "get married." Not exactly helpful. Disgusted, Fox went off alone. One day, when he had almost given up hope of encountering God in a way that the sacraments seemed to point to— experiencing the Real Presence of Christ—while reading his Bible, he heard a voice saying, "There is even one, Christ Jesus, who can speak to thy condition." It was a moment that turned his life outside in.

In the supreme confidence and strength of youth, George Fox began to "proclaim the day of the Lord" in the counties near his home. His message caught the attention of the Seekers. They rejoiced to hear that "Christ has come to teach His people Himself." They warmed to Fox's teaching of the immediacy of Christ's presence. They aligned themselves with his mission and went to work as the Publishers of Truth, Friends of Truth, Children of the Light, or simply Friends. Eventually, they called themselves the Religious

Society of Friends. They took that last name from a verse in the Gospel of John, where Jesus called His followers Friends.

Notice the adjective *Religious*. They weren't just some group gathered as a society of friends, people who liked each other. No, they gathered for spiritual purposes as the friends of Jesus. They took the John passage seriously, especially the part that said, "You are my friends if you do what I *command*" you [italics mine] and, "No longer do I call you servants, for the servant does not know what his master is doing; but I have called you friends, for all that I have heard from my Father I have made known to you." They wanted to hear Christ's call in their lives and learn from God directly.

Quietude Query

∽ Relax your body and mind.

∽ Breathe deeply.

∽ Put down the book.

∽ Think about the following Quietude Query slowly and gently. Savor each thought.

∽ What comes to mind when I think of the word "friend"? What does being a friend of Jesus mean to me?

To find the *Light* (one of their many metaphors for Jesus), these people felt the need for silence. They broke their silent worship only when someone felt a need to verbally share the Light that had shone in his or her soul. Sitting in silence, the people, now called *Quakers,* found their hearts filling with psalms, prayers, and hymns as they felt the Spirit of God move among and through them. Instead of dancing in the aisles with Pentecostal fervor, they knew in the stillness of their hearts the ecstatic love of Jesus. In silence, they encountered the sacrament of Christ's presence.

They didn't choose the nickname *Quaker,* by which Friends are best known today. The Puritans, and others, derisively called them Quakers because of their charac-teristic quaking during times of divine revelation. These early Friends did quake from time to time, both because they felt they were in the presence of the holy and because of the actual physical effect of the overpowering intensity of their message. They shook as a physical manifestation of the inner, silent work of the Spirit. They met Christ and witnessed, by word and deed, to the power and presence of the Christ they met in silence. Their lives spoke—and shook.

That witness is why Wilmer Cooper, a Friends theologian, writes:

> For more than three centuries Friends have had a testimony, which proclaims "the essentially spiritual nature of the believer's relationship to God." . . . The inward way of the Spirit is

believed not to be dependent upon outward rites, ceremonies, or liturgical aids to worship, but it is maintained that "the presence of Christ in the midst" can be a living experience for all who open themselves to the Spirit of God. This openness and living experience is achieved through silence.

Quakers believe that all of life is sacramental. For Friends, all occasions of life and every meal eaten holds the potential of becoming a sacred means of God's grace—if we prepare spiritually to see them as such, that is. Spiritual silence helps us prepare. That's what differentiates Quaker silence from non-Christian spiritual silences. Quaker silence anticipates the real presence of Christ coming in a sacramental way among and within us. In the holy hush we feed on Christ in our souls. As one group of Friends wrote, "In silence, without rite or symbol, we have known the Spirit of Christ so convincingly present . . . [that] this is our Eucharist and our Communion."

The Quaker view that all of life, including silence, is sacramental is grounded in the Bible as well as in Friendly faith. It is a practice solidly grounded in Christian theology, history, and Scripture. It's not a create-your-own-religion like the one described in "Worshipping Mr. Loh: Our personal deity is a 76-year-old Chinese guy" by Steve Silson. In his article Silson writes, "Since religions no longer depend upon location and culture; since one can be a Lutheran Buddhist, or a

Shiite Mormon, or a Neo-Pagan Universalist; since my wife and I both rejected the religions we were brought up with; since faith is now a matter of convenience rather than calling: Cathy and I have decided to ignore the existing religions altogether and worship our own personal deity. His name is Mr. Loh."

Mr. Loh is probably a very nice man. He may even be a holy man. But a deity? Too often such a god is the product of our own imaginations. This makes for some pretty small deities—especially when compared to the historic Christian imagination that has been grounded firmly in the Bible and in the lives of women and men for over 2,000 years. Quaker silence is rooted in Christian faith and practice that is larger than our own personal hopes, desires, and feelings. We know who that "You" is to whom we're praying: the God of Christian faith.

Christians believe that Jesus is God incarnate. Incarnation is an essential Christian doctrine that says God became human in the person of Jesus. This Jesus walked, talked, ate, slept, sweated, laughed, and cried in all the same ways we do. Jesus' touch made all things holy. He opened up our understanding of God and the ways of experiencing God. To explain God and the kingdom, He used the stuff of everyday life. God is like a loving father or a seeking shepherd, He said. He told how God's kingdom is like a mustard seed or leaven or a fishing net, all common things in His time made sacramental by Jesus' touch. Jesus showed us that the rich possibilities for meeting God are limitless.

Quietude Query

↜ Relax your body and mind.

↜ Breathe deeply.

↜ Put down the book.

↜ Think about the following Quietude Query slowly and gently. Savor each thought.

↜ Look around the space where I am now. Has anything in view ever felt sacramental to me? How or why?

Quakers are also urged to see God in the faces of others. Quaker founder George Fox urged us to "walk cheerfully over the world, answering that of God in everyone." As we do so, we encounter God in people, if our spiritual eyes are open to seeing the Divine that way.

I once put together a multimedia essay that I called "Christ in Commonlife." I planned to pair photographs I had taken of people with Bible verses—a modern-day illustrated Jesus. "Isn't this the carpenter?" from Mark's Gospel came alive as I photographed my sawdust-covered dad building a garage. A picture of my son Ben standing backlit gazing out on Cape Cod Bay illustrated, "And Jesus grew in wisdom and stature." As I stilled my soul and loaded my film, I found I saw Jesus in almost everyone. A project that I'd thought was going to be difficult, was easier than I anticipated. Taking good photographs and matching them with the right verses demanded careful attention, but it was easy, because I was looking for Him. I began seeing Jesus in the faces of folks around me. He was everywhere. He is everywhere. Silence helps us see that.

While seeing God in others and the things around us may sound pretty mystical, it is not mysticism for mysticism's sake. This mystical way of seeing the world and its people as part of the goodness of God comes from wanting to partake of the presence. We want to experience Jesus in our souls because, as the old folk hymn says:

Lord, I want to be a Christian in my heart, in my heart,
Lord, I want to be a Christian in my heart, in my heart.
In my heart, in my heart,
Lord, I want to be a Christian in my heart, in my heart.

Quaker silence helps us be a "Christian in our hearts" by showing us God's wants of us. When we see God's people and creation with spiritual eyes and a silent soul, we are flooded with the desire to live as the kind of women and men that we know in our hearts God wants us to be.

A friend of mine recently told me about such an encounter with God in silence. As she sat in silent waiting, she felt filled with an overwhelming sense of what God wanted her to do, and she received the power to do it. Included in God's word to her was an urging to be more loving. "I was amazed at how much more love I had for my husband," she said, "whom I already loved dearly. But I was even more amazed at how I could look at the formerly creepy panhandler outside the coffee shop with love, instead of my usual critical eye."

We want to know what God wants from us. This knowing what God wants is important because Quakers believe that faith and daily living are married. Holy silence infuses us with God's spirit and power so that we can live faithfully in life's common ventures: youth, adulthood, marriage, work, family, illness, and death. Each of us shares these, in some degree, with the rest of God's people. They are the normal stuff of life. Silence helps us to see that God is present in them. As English Friend William Littleboy wrote:

> God is above all the God of the normal. In the common facts and circumstances of life, He draws near to us, quietly. He teaches us in the routine of life's trifles, gently and unnoticed His guidance comes to us through the channels of 'reason [and] judgment.' . . . [W]e have been taught by Him when we least suspected it; we have been guided . . . though the guiding hand rested upon us so lightly that we were unaware of its touch.

This guiding hand resting lightly upon us is best felt when we are silent and still. Holy silence is intimately related to Friends' understanding of the Divine at work in the everyday. Carrie Newcomer expresses this in her song "Holy as a Day is Spent":

Holy is the dish and drain
The soap and sink, and the cup and plate
And the warm wool socks, and cold white tile
Showerheads and good dry towels
And frying eggs sound like psalms
With a bit of salt measured in my palm
It's all a part of a sacrament
As holy as a day is spent

Holy is the busy street
And cars that boom with passion's beat
And the check out girl, counting change
And the hands that shook my hands today
And hymns of geese fly overhead
And stretch their wings like their parents did
Blessed be the dog, that runs in her sleep
To catch that wild and elusive thing

Holy is the familiar room
And the quiet moments in the afternoon
And folding sheets like folding hands
To pray as only laundry can
I'm letting go of all I fear
Like autumn leaves of earth and air
For summer came and summer went
As holy as a day is spent

Holy is the place I stand
To give whatever small good I can
And the empty page, and the open book

Redemption everywhere I look
Unknowingly we slow our pace
In the shade of unexpected grace
And with grateful smiles and sad lament
As holy as a day is spent
And morning light sings "Providence"
As holy as a day is spent

Redemption, grace, and providence signifying God's active presence in our lives set Quaker silence apart from just being quiet. Newcomer's song reflects the Quaker belief that God is the God of the daily—and the daily reveals the deity. We best perceive this in times of holy hushes. Spiritual silence urges us to see God in a mustard seed and leaven and autumn leaves and smiling faces. It leads us into a new way of seeing, a way of seeing the invisible hand of God in all that we have been blessed with. Rufus Jones said, "We find Him when we enjoy beauty."

It's like when I see the Shaker box in our kitchen. In silence, I notice its simple beauty and remember the day I watched Charles Harvey making it. I remember his care. I see him hunched over his workbench, shaping the wood, setting the copper nails, and then signing his name and date to the bottom. Instead of just seeing a simply elegant, oval box, like our friends and family do when we're all gathered in the kitchen, I also see the trip that took Nancy and me to his shop in Berea, Kentucky. I bask in the love of that trip and meeting this artisan. I rejoice in Charles's handiwork and the blessing his work is in our lives, even a decade later.

That's what spiritual silence does. It helps us stop and sense God, the Creator, present in everyday life. We begin to see that the poetry of the Bible is more than poetry—"Then all the trees of the forest will sing for joy before the Lord, . . . give thanks to him and praise his name. For the Lord is good and his love endures forever." Singing trees, jubilant fields seem like poetic language. Trees don't sing and fields don't rejoice. Or do they? Could it be that the golden light that transforms field trash into something of beauty is a way the fields are being jubilant, reflecting God's light back to heaven? Could the graceful, waving naked limbs of trees be hands uplifted in praise to God? Maybe that's all a bit mystical, yet we each could use a bit of the Divine in our lives.

This appreciation for the divinely mysterious presence of God all around us is one of the things that makes Quaker silence holy. It helps us slow down and appreciate God's goodness to us. It enables us to see the Divine mark upon all of life's goodness—from maple Shaker boxes to fox squirrels in the maple trees. The amazing thing is that this silence is for every one—harried mother, busy businessperson, or frenetic teen.

Quaker silence enables men and women at any level of spiritual life to join in silent contemplation and worship whenever and wherever they are, physically and spiritually. For almost 400 years, ordinary people have been gathering together in silence and worshiping. In doing so they find themselves empowered to live well, and better, in the world.

This quiet, contemplative worship has another component that sets it apart from other spiritual silences. That is, "that brazen expectation [of hearing the voice of God] . . ." says writer Scott Russell Sanders. Quaker silence is filled with expectation—expectation that God will speak. When we hear God, our lives are changed.

Quietude Query

⤳ Relax your body and mind.

⤳ Breathe deeply.

⤳ Put down the book.

⤳ Think about the following Quietude Query slowly and gently. Savor each thought.

⤳ Have I ever expected to hear God's voice? How would I know if I heard it?

And, just as miraculous, because of hearing God's voice, those who gathered in silence find themselves melded into a spiritual community. As Ruth Fawell said, "As [silent] Meeting goes on, we may all be lifted together above our ordinary lives into a wonderful sense of unity and peace. . . . Our small separate lives, that before seemed like small boats, drifting along sluggishly or carried into the backwaters of wrongdoing and isolated there, are swept into the main current of God's purpose. We know that we have a place in God's purpose."

Early Friend Thomas Story, in his King James English, reports that when he attended silent worship with other Quakers:

> . . . not long after I had sat down among them, that heavenly and watery cloud over-shadowing my mind brake into a sweet abounding shower of celestial rain, and the greatest part of the meeting was broken together, dissolved, and comforted in the same divine and holy presence and influence of the true, holy, and heavenly Lord. . . . And, as the many small springs and streams descending into a proper place and forming a river become more deep and weighty, even so this meeting with a people gathered of the living God into a sense of the enjoyment of his divine and living presence.

Spiritual silence is available to everybody. Your faith tradition might have a practice of using silence in some unique way. This could be a good time to rediscover it and integrate it into what you're learning about Quaker silence. All holy silence, regardless of its origin, leads us to that "sweet abounding shower." As it washes over us, it blends us into God's flowing river of humanity, the body of Christ. Silence leads us to wait. Waiting leads us to the real presence of Jesus. The real presence leads us to holy awe. Holy awe leads us to a life lived out of spiritual silence. That life leads us to "unhurried peace and power," wrote Thomas Kelly. "It is simple. It is serene. It is triumphant. It is radiant. It takes no time, but it occupies all our time. . . . And when our little day is done we lie down quietly in peace, for all is well." Indeed, all manner of things are well.

CHAPTER THREE

A Thousand Clamoring Voices
Finding Silence in the Noise of Living

"True silence is the rest of the mind; and is to the spirit, what sleep is to the body, nourishment and refreshment." That's what William Penn said centuries ago. Many Americans think that the picture on the Quaker Oats box is a portrait of William Penn, for whom Pennsylvania was named. Except it's not and it wasn't. Pennsylvania was named for William's father, and nobody knows who the man on the oats box is.

William Penn was one of the first Friends. There are times that I think that he wrote the above quotation after seeing Friends snoring softly in Meeting. If, so, he's not the only one. Benjamin Franklin (who many people think was a Quaker because he dressed funny) writes about this happening on his first visit to Philadelphia. " . . . [I] walked again up the street, which by this time had many clean-dressed people in it, who were all walking the same way. I joined them, and thereby was led into the great meetinghouse of the Quakers near the market. I sat down among them, and, after looking round awhile and hearing nothing said, being very drowsy thro' labor and want of rest the preceding night, I fell fast asleep, and continued so till the meeting broke up, when one was kind enough to rouse me. This was, therefore, the first house I was in, or slept in, in Philadelphia."

In spite of that occurrence, which was not unique to Franklin, Penn probably had Jesus' statement in mind, "Come to me, all you who are weary and burdened, and I will give you rest." Who among us—mother, father, co-worker, boss—is not weary and burdened? Whose soul doesn't need nourishment and refreshment? Words and phrases like *burnout, chronic fatigue syndrome, stressed out* fill our conversations. Silence invites us to rest in God's loving care, a loving care so restful that some fall asleep.

Quietude Query

⌒ Relax your body and mind.

⌒ Breathe deeply.

⌒ Put down the book.

⌒ Think about the following Quietude Query slowly and gently. Savor each thought.

⌒ What nourishes my soul? Could silence be one of those things?

When we think about nourishment or refreshment, we usually think about food or fine restaurants or a good night's sleep or a vacation at the beach. That we could be nourished by silence isn't a thought that occurs to us. Aldous Huxley's 1946 statement that "Physical noise, mental noise and noise of desire . . . all the resources of our almost miraculous technology have been thrown into the current assault against silence," was eerily prescient. We fill our homes, offices, and cars with more and more sound.

I'm as guilty as anybody. I saw that clearly the day I scrambled to get speaker wire run through the walls and under the floor of our new house—in a rush to go golfing, on a Sunday, traditionally the day of rest, while writing a book on silence.

I appreciate silence. I value it. Silence restores my soul. But even a silence junkie like me needs to remember that spiritual silence takes effort and intentionality. Sometimes it is easier to work on rear speaker placement than it is to climb off the ladder in the dark, silent basement and listen for God's voice. I look around our new house and, even with our emphasis on silence, I see a competing emphasis on having sound—the right number of telephones, cable outlets, and speakers in strategic rooms. I put extra insulation in our bedroom ceiling and walls, but that had more to do with not hearing grandkids than for any spiritual purposes.

The way of silence isn't easy. Yet, it seems like it should be. After all, what is there to it? You just have to keep quiet. But that is sort of like saying, to a baby,

"C'mon and talk. It's easy. Just start." We need, as infants, to learn language if we want to communicate. To change our grunts and yelps and cries into words that adult ears recognize as "I'm hungry," "I need changing," or "Can I borrow the car and twenty dollars for gas?"

The same is true of silence. We need to learn its language. We learned to talk. Now we need to learn to listen. To be quiet. After years of people urging us to "Speak up," keeping our mouths shut and souls open can be like trying to shut off a faucet whose handle has broken off.

You might be one of those folks who find it easy to be quiet—a person who enjoys silence and solitude. Walking on a beach or living in a solitary apartment might be just your cup of contemplation. Silence, any kind of silence, may come naturally to you. If that's the case, then you have already begun the steps toward holy silence.

But then again you might be a person who finds silence difficult, or even unnerving. You might be like the man invited to a Quaker home for dinner. The meal started, as is Quaker custom, with silence. As he reported to some friends, "We sat down and there was this awkward silence. But then I told a little joke and broke the ice."

Many of us find it easier breaking the ice with a little joke or music than sitting in silence. If that's the case, then the way to holy silence can be a struggle. If you're one of those people, don't give up. Struggle is not failure.

My grandmother's piano sits in a corner of our living room. She played it "by ear"—never took a lesson in her life. I could expect, from her example, to walk over and begin to pick out notes, discern a pattern, and then play a one-finger tune, then add some more notes and finally bring in my left hand. I could expect that, but it wouldn't result in anything remotely musical. Playing the piano is hard for me. I have to have someone—a piano teacher or a boogie-woogie playing cousin—show me how to do it. I have to practice and practice and practice. Today I can play a little. Very little. It's a struggle, but it's not failure. No, it's not complete success, but the more I practice (if I practice) the better I get.

The same is true for silence.

One reason that being quiet is hard is that it's not a part of our lives. We're not used to it. We speed down the highway while chatting on cell phones. Wi-Fi in Starbucks lets us work instead of contemplating a cup of Joe and the day's blessings—holy in themselves.

We like noise because it shows action. Somebody's at work. Producing. Production can be commodified and priced. There's no way, though, to put a dollar value on soulful satisfaction. A counterfeit version of it exists. The busier we are, the more ego strokes we get from bosses and co-workers, and sometimes life partners. Most of these folks aren't going to congratulate us on time spent deepening our spiritual lives. They don't give bonuses for prayer.

Why? Because our spiritual lives are invisible, that's why. They can't be seen, measured, felt, or weighed. How do we judge if something is the way it is? "If it walks like a duck, smells like a duck, quacks like a duck, then it must be a duck"—and ducks are knowable. What if it doesn't walk, smell, or quack (or quake)? What is it then?

Our busyness and need to produce tangible results also infects activities that could lead us to contemplation—like gardening ("You got how many pansies planted!") or writing ("You've written how many books!"). That last one is, of course, my favorite, especially when it's exclaimed with the right amount of amazement. Here's the twist: When I'm writing at my best, my writing begins as an act of worship. It helps me grow silent. As my thoughts and feelings form themselves as words on a page, I begin to discover anew the ideas, dreams, and faith that matter most to me. In my writing silence, my faith comes alive. It strengthens me as I share myself. If, that is, I'm writing as a soulful activity instead of simply trying to meet a publishing deadline. Holy silence is hard for me.

Quietude Query

➣ Relax your body and mind.

➣ Breathe deeply.

➣ Put down the book.

⤳ Think about the following Quietude Query slowly and gently. Savor each thought.

⤳ Which takes a bigger place in my life—silence or noise? Which of the two do I feel more comfortable with?

Sometimes the Church is complicit in our busyness. If you search the Internet for successful congregations, you find lists of those that are large, active, and hosting seminars on being a "successful church." They build bigger buildings, design newer and more seeker-sensitive services, publish best-selling how-to books, and sponsor sold-out conferences. What they risk is losing a holy emphasis on being reflective, praying people of faith.

There is a place in the kingdom for large, active congregations, but not at the cost of silence and prayer. Christianity is a faith built on relationship—of people to God and to each other. Relationship is nurtured only with "face time," intimacy.

Jesus in the Gospels gave us an example. His life balanced action and times of reflection, prayerful solitude and compassionate ministry. Jesus alternated between times of inner nourishment and times of outward action. Both were faithful to God. The Church at its best helps us make more times for reconnecting with the Spirit of God.

When we're honest, though, we begin to admit that the busyness that we whine about (first it's soccer practice, then off to piano lessons, then back for a quick bite before we head to gymnastics, and off to Bible study) is also a way of stifling inner fears and anxieties.

Those fears and anxieties make silence scary. Especially for a people who, even if we don't watch Westerns anymore, have a collective, cinematic consciousness of a John Wayne-type hero peering up over the hill at a crucial point in a battle and saying, "I don't like it. It's too quiet out there." We know why it's quiet—the bad guys are just over the hill. They're getting ready to attack. If we're deep in contract negotiations at the office or trying to beat rush-hour traffic while cell-phoning the pizza place and placing our supper order, we don't have time to think about our fears. What happens if I lose my job, or where's the mortgage money coming from, or why am I forty years old and feeling like a failure? When it gets quiet, "too quiet," those thoughts swarm over our mental hills and attack us. We can hold them off when we're busy and vigilant. But when we're walking out alone to pick up the mail or lying in bed, they come to us unbidden. Then we become insomniacs, unable to rest for the thoughts crowding us. We don't know how to be quiet. We don't know how to sit in silence with the big questions of our lives. We don't know how to ask God to lead us. So we stay noisy and busy.

I'm in a hotel while I'm writing this section of the book. Stuck in one of the drawers of the TV armoire is a little flyer that asks, "Did work come to bed with you again? Already watched the late, late show? And that darn Sandman is still not here? Just dial O to have a CD player and relaxation CD delivered to your room!" The exclamation point at the end is perfect, screaming at me to relax.

The desert fathers saw busyness as moral laziness. These men, a sort of early Common Era protest movement, urged people to learn the way of silence because it leads us back to our true selves. Silence steers us inward, to the secret places of our souls. Once there, it directs us to worship God and consider the meaning of our lives in the light of Jesus' call to follow Him. Quaker silence continues this tradition.

If we are never silent, then we never have to look at the truth about ourselves. Noise keeps me from confronting my snapping at my co-worker over his perceived inattention to budget forecasting. Noise lets me avoid dwelling on how I cut someone off on the freeway, and then shot her a dirty look, like it was her fault.

Spiritual silence, on the other hand, is a scalpel. It slices our souls open. It cuts through the layers of our fears and insecurities and our reliance on ourselves instead of God. It lays open to spiritual diagnosis our lack of trust and faith. Just as surgery can be scary, so, too, can silence. Especially at first. Silence leads us to a self-discovery of any sin hidden deep within us. I'm not talking about big sins. I'm talking about the little sins that hold us back from being the people we feel deep in our souls God wants us to be. The little sin of cutting off our teenagers in mid-explanation about why they missed curfew. Or giving a dollar instead of a ten to a panhandler or five minutes instead of an hour to an annoying, needy neighbor. So long as we're busy, we can sing along with Todd Snider:

> I think I'm an alright guy
> I know I ain't perfect but God know I try

Holy silence cuts through that obfuscation. It shows us that that we are not "alright guys." And then it helps us begin to deal with it. In silence we discover God-led answers for being better listeners, less stingy with our time and money, and our other felt failings. Our success-oriented world won't lead us to worry about those kinds of things. Successories, the motivational poster people, encourages action, not contemplation. Their "unique collection of themed merchandise is designed to promote a positive outlook, celebrate human achievement, and inspire excellence in your career, your business, and your life." They tell us over and over again—in posters and desk accessories and computer screen-savers—that, "Every day in every way we're getting better and better." We know, when we're spiritually silent, that we're not. That's what makes silent spiritual self-examination painful—which may be why there aren't many desert fathers today. Or Quakers.

Silence is also painful, and sometimes scary, because we don't trust it long enough to fully experience it. Unlike surgery, where most scalpels are used, we are not anesthetized during silence. We feel each cut. And so we rush through it. That's true even in the most solemn of occasions. I recently attended an event where the emcee announced that we would have a moment of silence in memory of the previous year's speaker (he had died right after the last conference). "Let's have a moment of silence for George Plimpton," the emcee intoned, "and," with scarcely a nanosecond of silence, "in other announcements. . . . " I admit I'm accustomed to momentary pauses in public places being passed off as moments of silence. But the extreme brevity of this moment caught me by surprise.

Spiritual examination is a goal of Quaker silence. At its most basic, it can be as simple as using the silence as a time of asking questions about ourselves. Do I see my time, talents, energy, and money, as gifts from God? Do I buy more stuff because I need it, or to impress my neighbors or myself? Do I eat too much so I'll feel less empty inside? Am I truthful at all times? Do I treat others fairly? Do I recognize the needs and the gifts of everybody in my family? Even that really pesky relative?

You can make up your own questions to use in silent self-examination. Let them provide a framework in which to prayerfully consider your life's direction. As we've seen, not all of these questions are easy. Still, by facing them in the holy hush, they can lead us into healing.

Quietude Query

⌒ Relax your body and mind.

⌒ Breathe deeply.

⌒ Put down the book.

⌒ Think about the following Quietude Query slowly and gently. Savor each thought.

⌒ What self-examination questions do I need to ask?

Quakers call the presence of the Holy Spirit working within us a "sifting silence." It separates the worthwhile from the worthless. Since we sometimes confuse those two—we may know what we value, but what we value may not be valuable. It can be a disturbing experience. Sometimes silence even shows us that the choice is not between what is wrong and what is right, but between what is right and what is right *for us*. While in the beginning some spiritually silent, self-examination is painful, it can grow into a silence that is deeply rewarding. If you can only handle a nanosecond of silence, that's okay. Begin there. Squirm. Try to find a comfortable place in an uncomfortable stillness. Then try for two nanoseconds. Then two real seconds. Two minutes. Ten minutes. Holy silence is a way of exploring the deep riches of the interior life, including the soul's discomfort with its failings, and asking God for help. It is a way of confession and reconciliation—a road into sacramental living.

That's what makes this clearing work deeply loving. "Just because we feel in turmoil," says David Runcorn in

The Center of Quiet, ". . . does not mean that God is too. . . . The neglect of our inner world may mean that a lot of suppressed energy is locked up within us. Its strength and vigor can be alarming when we meet it for the first time."

We can shutter our souls with activity, but powerful spiritual silence, if we allow it, will blow fresh winds of the Spirit through us. Not like a safe spring breeze. More like the hurricane. When the power of God comes to us in holy silence we might be blown about, or even blown apart.

The important thing to remember as we experience spiritual silence is that it doesn't leave us in pain and turmoil. That's what the prophet Elijah discovered in the still, small voice. Hearing God in the whisper renewed him. Holy silence leads us into the contemplation of true faith. What does Christ's call on our life mean? How does that affect my life as a father, a boss, a husband, or a so-so golfer? Holy silence is a gift that gives us time to carefully think about the most important life matters—family, friends, work, and God. Theological or religious discussions about esoterica or hidden texts or the nature of what Jesus actually said might interest academicians and some professional clergy, but the rest of us want help for the living of these days. How can we be the people God wants us to be—the people that we feel deep in our bones and souls that we want to be? How can I be the best father to my children when I feel like I don't know what I'm doing and I feel I'm only a half step in front of them on life issues?

I need God's help. That's why holy silence is an important part of Quaker life. It's not just some quirky denominational doctrinal add-on that we created in the seventeenth century. Quakers see holy silence as so central to Christianity that we can't contemplate faith without it. It is crucial to the life of faith. The early Friends believed and taught that Jesus comes to teach His people Himself. It's what Quakers mean when they refer to the *Inner Light*. Jesus' Spirit lives in and illuminates our lives. In the first century, he taught His followers on the roads and hillsides of Galilee. Today His Spirit communes with our spirit. In this silence, the ever-living Christ leads us into a contemplation of the holy.

The vistas of our souls open up when we sit silent before God. As we remove ourselves from the center of our existence and focus on the Divine, we encounter the creative mystery that is God. Silent centering prepares us for the gift of God's presence. We center ourselves in quiet contemplation, with God at our center. We are humbled in this presence. In this silence, it is difficult to stay self-centered. We are led into reflection, into life's deepest questions: Why am I here, what is my purpose, what should I do? Using spiritual silence to reflect on Jesus' phrases such as *take up my cross, love one another*, and *turn the other cheek* helps us think about how we live those directives out at work with a pushy boss or at home with kids, yard-work, and a spouse all clamoring for attention. Holy silence leads us into the presence of Jesus where He asks us, like He did the apostle Peter, "Do you love me?" and we reply, "Yes, Lord, you know we do," and then He says, "Feed my sheep." Silence helps me answer what it means for me to feed Jesus' sheep. How do I do that when I'd rather not deal with that smelly, ragged homeless guy who sits on the bench outside my office while I'm on my way to the new Scottish restaurant for lunch? What *would* Jesus do? Such a question deserves to be answered with more than a woven bracelet or bumper sticker. It demands patient, holy silence.

Helping us think about such questions is what makes holy silence a "school for faithfulness," as Quaker writer John Punshon describes it. Silence shows us that lives of justice, peace, truth, and equality answer such questions. Silence leads us into the life of ministry to which Jesus calls us. On the surface, social justice and peace may seem to be left-leaning political positions. But in Quaker life they are simply seen as commands rising out of the silence. When we are silent, we hear the voice of the One who says, "You are my friends if you do what I command you." And we begin to reflect on His teaching. We wonder, what does He command? Then we remember the words we've read in the Bible. Things like, "You have already been told what is right and what Yahweh wants of you. Only this, to do what is right, to love loyalty and to walk humbly with your God."

Holy silence calls us to our better selves—to lives of justice, kindness, and humility, and walking with God. Not just globally, either. Personally—to treat our family members kindly, deal fairly with business associates, let someone cut in front of us in line and not get mad, and take time for God.

Quietude Query

⤖ Relax your body and mind.

⤖ Breathe deeply.

⤖ Put down the book.

⤖ Think about the following Quietude Query slowly and gently. Savor each thought.

⤖ The prophet Micah says that God requires us to "act justly and to love mercy and to walk humbly with your God." What do I think God requires of me?

Silence, not words, leads us aright. "I have never repented of silence," said St. Arsenius. I know I have often mourned words that passed my lips. Often, in silence, I remember words I wish I could take back. I've said many things that I know, when I am silent, were not reflections of Jesus, but sprang from my need to best someone verbally or overwhelm them with my intellect. Spiritual silence reminds me that I need to be still and learn from the One who placed ego aside—even though it led to a cross. In the holy silence we come to know the living Word, as the Gospel writer of John calls Jesus. This life and light of humankind still shines in the darkness. In the silence we come to the Living Word of God directly—the Word that the writer of Hebrews tell us ". . . is living and active, sharper than any two-edged sword, piercing to the division of soul and spirit, of joints and marrow, and discerning the thoughts and intentions of the heart." Silence takes us to a place in our souls where we stand naked in spirit before God—guilty, then forgiven, and finally blameless. All our secrets are laid bare to God's eyes and our own. God then gives us the power to see ourselves as we truly are. In the silence I often have to face the fact that I am not nearly so nice a guy as I usually think I am. I see when I've been mean-spirited or apathetic. I remember the times I shot nasty looks at people who jumped in front of me at the grocery store checkout.

Silence doesn't leave me there, though. In holy silence God begins giving me the power to live my faith. In silence I see God's work in me being slowly realized. Any time any of us come into God's presence we leave ready to live out the gospel with as much light as we have been given. That is, if we take time, and not just a quick hit of silence, to be still.

When first we sit in silence, after we clear the noise in our own heads, we begin to notice how unsilent the world is. This awareness can be a source of frustration— "Why don't they shut up?" or "Why's he have that bass booming so loud in his car?"—or learning. Tayeko Yamanouchi shows how hearing the noise around us can be turned for good, once we learn to be silent.

As I silence myself I become more sensitive to the sounds around me, and I do not block them out. The songs of the birds, the rustle of the wind, children in the playground, the roar of an airplane overhead are all taken into my worship. . . . I think of myself like the tree planted by the "rivers of water" in Psalm 1, sucking up God's gift of life and being restored.

"Sucking up God's gift of life and being restored" in silence. That's why George Fox urged us to "Carry some quiet around inside thee. Be still and cool in thy own mind and spirit, from thy own thoughts, and then thou wilt feel the principle of God to turn thy mind to the Lord from whence cometh life; whereby thou mayest receive the strength and power to allay all storms and tempests."

How do we ever learn to carry quiet around inside us, unless we take time for silence? We need silence for times of reflection and renewal. We need times of quieting our racing hearts and minds, and listening for the voice of God. If, that is, we are going to learn to respond to God who ever reaches out to us. We need silent, stopping times.

Silent, stopping times are harder to bring about than they are to just think about. All our good intentions will not make them happen, even if we know we need them. This is what Martin Hope Sutton, a British Friend and co-founder of one of Britain's major seed and gardening companies, discovered, writing eloquently that:

> . . . God was waiting in the depths of my being to talk to me if I would only get still enough to hear His voice.

I thought this would be a very easy matter, and so I began to get still. But I had no sooner commenced than a perfect pandemonium of voices reached my ears, a thousand clamoring notes from without and within, until I could hear nothing but their noise and din. Some of them were my own voice, some of them were my own questions, some of them were my own cares, some of them were my very prayers. Others were the suggestions of the tempter and the voices of the world's turmoil. Never before did there seem so many things to be done, to be said, to be thought; and in every direction I was pushed and pulled, and greeted with noisy acclamations of unspeakable unrest. It seemed necessary for me to listen to some of them, and to answer some of them; but God said, "Be still, and know that I am God." Then came the conflict of thoughts for the morrow, and its duties and cares; but God said, "Be still." And as I listened and slowly learned to obey, and shut my ears to every sound, I found after awhile that when the other voices ceased, or I ceased to hear them, there was a still, small voice in the depths of my being that began to speak with an inexpressible tenderness, power, and comfort. As I listened, it became to me the voice of prayer, and the voice of wisdom, and the voice of duty, and I did not need to think so hard, or pray so hard, or trust so hard, but that "still, small voice" of the Holy Spirit in my heart was God's prayer in my secret soul, was God's answer to all my questions, was God's life and strength for soul and body, and became the substance of all knowledge, and all prayer, and all blessing; for it was the living God Himself as my life and my all.

Once we immerse ourselves in silence, then we may feel, for a while at least, like we are in the path of a dam that has burst. A life cluttered with accumulations of years of hopes and fears, plans and ideas, light and darkness needs space. In silence the Holy Spirit clears a space. We need to become like "The House at Rest" in Jessica Power's poem:

> The house must first of all accept the night.
> Let it erase the walls and their display,
> impoverish the rooms till they are filled
> with humble silences; let clocks be stilled
> and all the selfish urgencies of day. . . . .
>
> Virtue it is that puts a house at rest.
> How well repaid that tenant is, how blest
> who, when the call is heard,
> is free to take his kindled heart and go.

Silence doesn't cure all our ills, spiritual and otherwise. After years of practicing silence, I am still impatient with other drivers, get anxious when my schedule doesn't go as I think it should, and am fearful while flying. Still, how much more mean-spirited, anxious, or fearful might I be if I didn't practice holy silence?

Holy silence is there for us anytime we need or want it. If I shut off NPR on my way to work, I find that silence is in the car with me on my morning commute. As I relax into the shower after splitting wood on a fall day, I feel it in the spray around me. All I need do is take it in. As I do, I find myself thinking more clearly and feel my spirit being renewed. I feel tension easing from my mind and muscles. Slowly, my life transforms—I feel a slight smile at work well done or I finally figure out how to deal with that annoying problem at work, by the presence of God in and with me. The only explanation for that transformation, subtle or dramatic, is that I took time to listen for the still, small voice of God.

Silence also helps carve out oases of peace in the midst of hectic family life. It can be a time out for our families' souls. I'm not foolish enough to suggest that you gather your family at an appointed time and sit in a silent circle in the living room. I am foolish enough, as a young parent, to have tried that . . . only to have everybody rebel. It was not a pretty sight, nor one of my finest parental moments.

Still, families can practice spiritual silence in practical ways. These ways can be as simple as inviting everybody to pause while piling into the car to "take a breath" before backing out of the garage or to bow heads in silent prayer at meal times—taking a Quaker "grace."

This grace is an action everybody can participate in, youngest to oldest, verbal or silent. Instead of always talking to—or more likely, at—God, it becomes more a time of listening. This is a way to teach children how to listen with their spiritual as well as their outer ears. These short pauses encourage them to be faithful to the movings of the Spirit in the same way young Samuel was. The holiness of the moment is revealed in their soul's intent to know and be known by God.

Quietude Query

⤢ Relax your body and mind.

⤢ Breathe deeply.

⤢ Put down the book.

⤢ Think about the following Quietude Query slowly and gently. Savor each thought.

⤢ Imagine my family being creatively quiet. How could that happen and what would it look like?

Silence is also a way to minister to those in need. Many times as a pastor I've been called to difficult situations—a schizophrenic kid who had threatened his parents or a church member who was seemingly on the mend and then suddenly dying in the hospital too far ahead of her time. On occasions such as these, I have heard other people say some insensitive things. I have said such things, too. Then one day I read from St. Arsenius, "I

have often repented of speech, but never of silence." You'll remember that I quoted him earlier. *Hmm*, I wondered, *was this man an early voice for Quakers like me?* What he said reminds us to stay silent and be caring. In many situations silence helps the person we're with more than words can. We bring more comfort to their soul by keeping quiet than by filling the void with words. This is especially true in crucial life and death moments.

Many of us find it hard to visit folks who are seriously ill or dying. Yet, we know in our soul that we need to make such a visit. Part of our anxiety comes from worrying about what to say—or being fearful that we'll say something wrong or stupid or hurtful. Words often rush in where feelings fear to walk. "Hush, hush," says the angel in Shlomo DuNour's novel *Adiel,* "lest you cause pain to your friend. Even in loving words there is the power to hurt and to wound. Silence is best when the ways of the Lord are hidden from our eyes."

Many things lie hidden from our eyes, especially the reasons for illnesses or emotional pain or death. We cannot comprehend these afflictions or why they happen. The holy gift of Quaker silence offers help in our questioning—and not just to us personally. Holy silence gives us a way to be with others, helping them wrestle with the large questions of life—*why this, why me, why them, why now, why God?* Silence may not give an answer, but silence provides a safe place with a friend and God.

"Quakers do have something very special to offer the dying and the bereaved," writes Diana Lampen. " . . .

namely that we are at home in silence. Not only are we thoroughly used to it and unembarrassed by it, but we know something about sharing it, encountering others in its depths and, above all, letting ourselves be used in it."

Sharing spiritual silence with another person who dwells in that soulful space where words don't matter, sustains the invisible, eternal bond of love and God. It moves us into the eternal mystery beyond verbal expression. Only the soul, not the mind, can express our deepest feelings.

What matters most in my hardest times is simply having somebody sit with me. I don't care if he or she speaks or not. The being there is enough. Holding silence with me is more helpful than Hallmark sentiments or pious prayers. In the dark days of a divorce, the friends I relied on most were the ones who didn't worry about words of consolation or condemnation, but were simply present.

Such sensitivity to spiritual silence leads us to help others, even in the most difficult situations. That's why Roger J. Vanden Busch wrote, "Quakers find in silence a deepening process bringing us into our hearts where we meet God, are empowered, and finally led to the service of others."

Quietude Query

🖜 Relax your body and mind.

🖜 Breathe deeply.

⊱ Put down the book.

⊱ Think about the following Quietude Query slowly and gently. Savor each thought.

⊱ Have I ever shared silence with someone in need? What made it feel like the thing to do?

Silence, especially in life's busyness, leads us through the whitewater of life to gentle pools of stillness and calm. Almost four hundred years of Quaker silence have pointed us back to the center within. Silence moves us from difficult self-examination, to healing, to relaxing in God's presence. Interior silence takes us to a place where we are living St. Paul's injunction to pray without ceasing, even when we are not consciously aware that we are doing so. That happened to me on a recent Good Friday. I spent the day hammering the nails out of pieces of wood from the pallets that the outside walls of our new house had come on. Our home is made of timbers recycled from old factories, and the exterior walls were constructed on jigs on the factory floor. These were then put on pallets and shipped on semis from New Hampshire to our Indiana home site. "The wood we use in the pallets is better than most builders use in their homes," said one of the people building our house. "You'll want to salvage as much of it as you can. Don't let the framers burn it up."

Quakers are strong on grace and redemption. If something can be saved and used again, it is. I hoped to see these used two-by-fours "born again" as a woodshed or a workshop. So, the sun blazed and I pounded nails out instead of in. A few yards away, four framers worked at pounding nails in, hanging the walls and roof panels. While I drove 16 commons out of two-by-fours, they drove ten- and twelve-inch spikes through two-by-six walls into six-inch posts and beams with three pound sledges. The sound of hammers on nails rang through the Good Friday afternoon. That ringing was accompanied by the church bells from St. Thomas More Catholic Church just a couple of miles away, drifting on the spring breeze.

This symmetry with the holy day was not lost on me, even though Friends, being non-liturgical, don't celebrate holy days or seasons. Still it was easy to recall other nails driven long ago—not through walls into posts, but through outstretched hands into rough wood. Even while carpenters yelled to each other, rough voices calling out measurements and grunting and cursing to set panels in place, I found silence in my soul. I was not sitting in a congregation listening to the last words of Jesus. Nor was I following the Stations of the Cross. But I was, in my soul, remembering, alongside those congregants. My arms grew weary of pounding and pulling nails. In, but at the same time apart from, the noise I pondered Jesus' tiring journey that day. In spite of the noise, silence swathed my soul. *Here I am,* I thought, *spending Good Friday in the company of carpenters. How fitting.* I prayed for them. I prayed for me. I prayed for the world.

I heard a car pull up our long lane. It was my friend Aaron. A rabbi. My soul laughed—*how right, how good.*

Carpenters and a rabbi on Good Friday. I thanked God for the silence of my soul that helped me to see that that day was holy because God breathed life into it.

I was led into the holy that day, while hammering out nails and visiting with rabbis and framers. Arms weary, back bent from stacking reclaimed wood, I found it was a Good Friday.

CHAPTER FOUR

SoulCare
Practical Steps Toward Silence

The television blares. People are talking so loudly that I feel like my head will implode from the noise. Loudness doesn't always bother me. Sometimes it feels right—like when revving my MG getting ready for a ride in the country. Or sitting in the front row at a jazz concert. Or at our local high school's football game—"Go, fight, Quakers!" But tonight's loudness is not right. This noise seems constant. As it has been for me for the past three months. My wife, Nancy, began caring for her ailing ninety-three-year-old father a few years ago, and for the last year she's lived at his farmhouse. I stayed at our quiet, if lonely, house in town. When it was sold as part of the preparations for building our new home, I needed a place to live. So I moved out to the farm with Nancy. Good. And her dad. Not so good.

Nancy's dad is an irascible old farmer. His disposition hasn't improved with age. Added to that is he's getting more and more hard of hearing. His only form of diversion other than constantly calling for Nancy to bring him water, popcorn, or help him pee is watching television. His increasing deafness means that the television has to be turned up really loud. You have to yell to be heard over it. The noise is compounded when visitors drop in to see him. They yell, too, to be heard over the TV.

On this particular night, my brother-in-law hollers at Nancy's dad and he's hollering back and John Wayne hollers out of the TV at them. I'm sitting in the corner trying to do a crossword puzzle. Usually I can get lost in silent words like these. But tonight it's impossible. I feel my soul suffocating. I need a quiet place. And I know where to find one. Dodging gunshots, verbal and televised, I head upstairs to our bedroom.

My Friendly faith has taught me to recognize my need for silence—as well as ways to find silence, even in the midst of great noise. My faith has taught me that I do not have to be on a silent retreat deep in a monastery. Silence takes me on an interior retreat. I've learned that I do not have to be imbued with Zen-like natural grace. Silence teaches me contemplation. I've seen that I don't have to find a Meetinghouse. Silence turns my soul into a sanctuary. This holy hush is realized even in the din and drone of everyday life. It can find me when I am surrounded by daily noise. It can find you, too.

The first thing I know to do when the television's turned up too loud, is take some time for soulcare. The apostle Paul's exhortation "not to think of yourself more highly than you ought to think," also carries the subtle suggestion that we should think *rightly* of ourselves. Part of that right thinking is learning to care for ourselves.

I'm a type-A personality, if God ever made one, which has made this a hard lesson for me. Much of my life has been spent trying to accomplish everything at work and home better and more quickly than anybody else could. I had important work as a spouse, father, friend, minister, administrator, and all-around great guy. I needed to take care of other people and situations. That didn't leave me with a lot of time to worry about taking care of myself. *If I was doing God's work,* I reasoned, *wouldn't God take care of me?* That's what the old gospel song promises—

> God will take care of you
> through ev'ry day, o'er all the way;
> God will take care of you
> God will take care of you.

Who was I to doubt those well-sung words?

Yet, there were times that God didn't seem to be fulfilling God's end of the deal. At least not in any ways I perceived. I was often impatient, especially with other people's driving habits. I experienced time pressure acutely—how will I ever clear this stuff off my desk and get the yard mowed before dark? I generally felt driven and wondered why. The gospel song promised, "All you may need He will provide, God will take care of you." Where was that care? Finally, because sometimes I get so busy that I forget the obvious, it occurred to me to look at Jesus. After all, if God was going to take care of anybody, it'd have to be Jesus. That's when I discovered that, on one level, God took care of Jesus by Jesus taking care of Jesus. That level was Jesus using silence.

Examples of Jesus' practicing silence as part of a spiritual discipline of self-care fill the Gospels. In Matthew 14 we read the story of Jesus' taking five loaves of bread and two fishes and feeding a multitude, and having twelve baskets of leftovers. A crowd had followed Him along the seashore after finding out that He had climbed into a boat for some quiet time. The throng was waiting for Him when He stepped ashore. He was concerned for them and for their need. So He began healing "their sick," as the New Jerusalem Bible says. In need of healing, they came to Jesus with hopeful hearts. Jesus healed them. He spent so much time attending to the needs that it soon grew dark. The people were hungry. So Jesus blessed the loaves and fishes and fed them. Then He went for a walk on the water. Real type-A personality sorts of behavior—busy, busy, busy. We remember those stories. But there's an important story between them—it takes up only one verse and so often gets overlooked. The verse reads, "After he had dismissed them, he went up on a mountainside by himself to pray. When evening came, he was there alone." Jesus could have hopped back on the boat with the rest of disciples and allowed Himself to be swept up in the needs of the people at the next landing. But He didn't. He stepped back. He made space to be alone. He found time to be silent. In so doing, He took care of His spirit. This silence of solitary prayer and worship prepared Him for His next miracle—walking on the water and inviting Peter to walk with Him.

Mark's Gospel opens with a flurry of messianic activity: Jesus is tested in the wilderness; begins preaching; calls the first four disciples; and cures a demoniac, Simon's mother-in-law, and a whole passel of other folks. That's all in the first chapter. Again, type-A busyness. Then, tucked away in a verse just before the chapter closes, we read, "Very early in the morning, while it was still dark, Jesus got up, left the house and went off to a solitary place, where he prayed."

Most of us miss that verse. But verses like it and the one in Matthew show us that Jesus knew that taking silence in the midst of busyness was a part of soulcare. Times like these were essential for the care and feeding of His soul. If I want to model my life after Jesus', then I have to take time to care for my soul. Still, soulcare has been a lifetime of learning when I need silence.

I've wondered if Jesus felt signals that told Him it was time for silence. If He did, then maybe I can learn them from His example, too. Looking back at the Matthew story, we find that the reason He climbed into the boat in the first place was that He had heard the awful news of His cousin's death. He needed quiet time, but it didn't work out the way He planned. The need persisted, and He cleared space for silence later, after He had healed the sick and fed the hungry.

If Jesus sensed the need for silence, then I need to learn how to sense this need, too. Now, after years of ignoring them, the warning signs that outside words and activity are becoming too much are pretty clear to me. I feel my muscles getting tight or aching. My posture stiffens. I walk or talk (or both) too fast. Little things irritate me. As a diabetic, I find those same things happening when my blood sugar is low. So if they don't go away when I eat a piece of fruit or a cookie, I know I need some non-action. Sometimes, when I'm not taking care of myself, all the noise and stress and driving myself leads to a full blown panic attack—the kind where I can't breathe, and I can convince myself I'm having a heart attack.

Quietude Query

⤺ Relax your body and mind.

⤺ Breathe deeply.

⤺ Put down the book.

⤺ Think about the following Quietude Query slowly and gently. Savor each thought.

⤺ What are my "silence signals"?

When I'm smart enough, or aware enough, to feel these things happening, then that's when I need to *hold silence,* as Quakers say. We don't say, "be silent." We *hold* it in our souls as carefully as a baby bird in our hands. Gently, softly. That's because, like a baby bird, holy silence can be easily crushed. This eliminates the possibility of its growing into something that fills us with love for God and healing the hurts we've carried into the silence.

Holding something lightly takes real attention. It's easy to grasp firmly. You just hold on tight. But to hold lightly means to watch what you're doing, to be aware of your grip, the pattern your hands make, and the pressure you're applying. Holy silence calls for that same sort of holding lightly, giving attention from the deepest resources of your being. That's because it's not just sitting still. It's not just not speaking. It's a wide-awake, full awareness. Held this way, silence feeds our souls as we feel ourselves being filled with a sense of God's closeness and care.

I didn't learn the way of silence by sitting through long hours in Meeting for Worship as a kid. I have friends who did. They tell me that some of those hours lasted for days. And they were never given any good explanation about how and why silence is good for them, except in the way that broccoli is good for them. They didn't particularly care for broccoli either.

I did grow up a Quaker, but of the "noisy" variety—in a Meeting that had a paid pastor and a Sunday bulletin, that sang hymns and heard sermons. We had silence, but it was usually short. But even those short silences spoke to my soul.

Real encounters with holy silence began for me at Wilmington College, a small Quaker school in southeastern Ohio. There, through wise and loving professors, I was called home to Quakerism—though of a more silent kind than the one I had grown up in. I drew nearer to the power of silence, understanding how it was both healing and hopeful. It became something that I welcomed. In the midst of studies and my work as a youth pastor, I yearned for silence like I yearned for cool water on a hot, humid Ohio day. As I went through college and seminary I became more grounded in silence through experiencing its power at Meetings for Worship.

Most of us, though, don't have to go through all of that to learn the way of holy silence. There are simple practices that can lead us into the path of silence without needing to go to seminary or seek out a Quaker meeting. Some of them sound simple. Others are similar to ways of learning meditative breathing. Regardless of their simplicity (especially for those of us who like things hard) and familiarity (to those who distrust the familiar), they are ways into holy silence.

Silence begins with expectation—the expectation of encountering God. Holy silence is just not an exercise in clearing your thoughts or finding a little peace and quiet. Peace and quiet may come, but they will come as a result of having been in the presence of the ever-living, ever-loving Christ. One incentive for getting away from earthly noise and human voices is to hear the Voice from Heaven. Remember those earlier Bible stories of Elijah, Habakkuk, and Paul?

They were confident that in silence God would make God's self known. They believed that God communed with those who sought Him. They expected that if they were quiet and still (and these two aren't always the same—we've all known kids at church who may have been quiet but were far from still) that they would receive a word from God. They believed that God would speak. God did. God still does—in a direct and living way. If we want to clearly hear the divine voice speaking within us, then we need to be still. We need to be silent in the center of our souls. That way God's presence becomes real and is a part of us.

In the same way that Elijah expected to hear God in the thunder, earthquake, fire, and lightning, but discovered God in the still, quiet voice, Thomas Kelly reminds us that "There is a divine Abyss within us all, a holy Infinite Center, a Heart, a Life who speaks in us and through us to the world. We have all heard this holy Whisper at times." By holding silence lightly and expectantly, we hear the voice of God. God still speaks in holy whispers. We hear them best in spiritual silence. When we are quiet and expectant, God takes the initiative. Isaac Pennington urged Friends, "So, be still and quiet, and silent before the Lord, not putting up any request to the Father, nor cherishing any desire in thee, but in the Seed's lowly nature and purely springing life; and the Lord give thee the clear discerning, in the lowly Seed, of all that springs and arises in thy heart." It's old-fashioned language, but timeless truth. We need to sit silently and expectantly so God can speak to our heart's condition, no matter its condition. We may arrive feeling joyous and leave finding ourselves filled with greater joy. That's what happened to Nancy and me in Vermont. We'd been on one of our best vacations ever and it was hard to think how it could be better. But in the silence of worship, God flooded the room and our souls, leaving no room for anything but joy.

Or, we may be troubled, and God will speak a word of peace that soothes our hearts and souls. I often felt overwhelmed with loneliness in the early days of my divorce. I especially missed my two sons, who lived in a city an hour away from me. Driving to make a business call, I'd pull to the side of the road and wait silently while the semis zipped by. *A word,* I'd pray, *just a word to calm this hurt.* Often a word came—sometimes in a feeling of peace settling like a blanket over me. Other times, it was remembering a scrap of Scripture—"Peace! Be still!" And, like the troubled sea and howling wind that Jesus first spoke those words to, my soul would settle. The missingness was still there, but through God's presence, it became bearable.

Joy, peace, and more come to us from God's voice as we wait in expectant silence.

Quietude Query

⇆ Relax your body and mind.

⇆ Breathe deeply.

⇆ Put down the book.

⇆ Think about the following Quietude Query slowly and gently. Savor each thought.

⇆ What would it feel like to wait expectantly, with body, mind, and heart?

As we learn the way of holy silence—a silence that expects to encounter and hear God—we begin finding our spirits in continuous communion with God. This can be true even when life rushes around us—even a noisy night like the one I experienced with my father-in-law's too-loud TV. Silence shows us that we can live at different levels. We can be outwardly busy, while inwardly talking and listening to God. We can be changing the oil in our car or cooking supper or giving a presentation at work, while at the same time, if we practice the way of holy silence, we can be centered in our souls and in communion with Christ. Thomas Kelly, one of the great guides of the interior life, urges us toward inner, silent contemplation by saying that it is a way " . . . of conducting our inward life so that we are perpetually bowed in worship, while we are also very busy in the world of daily affairs. . . . This practice is the heart of religion. It is the secret, I am persuaded, of the inner life of the Master of

Galilee. He expected this secret to be freshly discovered in everyone who would be His follower."

When we discover the secret of being inwardly at worship while outwardly at work, we find that the soul's silence brings us to God and God to us. Silence takes us beyond the limits of consciousness and into the heart and mind and will of God. Instead of our possessing God through silence, God through silence possesses us.

While our goal, as people seeking the holy, is to be in constant communion with God, there are some times that holy silence calls for a specific space and time. When that's the case, we will be drawn to make a place where that can happen. You may need to be creative, especially if you're not in your own home, like me while staying at my father-in-law's farm. It was his space—his house. My space was Nancy's and my bedroom. It was up and away from where her father spent most of his time. I couldn't hear the TV there.

Only you know where your best place will be. If you live alone, it may be your whole house. If you have a family, it may be one quiet corner. Whatever it is, look for a place that warms your soul and is handy. Yes, it would be nice to be able to zip to the quiet of a Meetingroom or be like the old-world *riche* and have our own private chapel. But that's not realistic. Or necessary. We make rooms for watching television. Why not for communing with God?

Such a space doesn't need stained glass windows and statuary. In fact, if you wanted it to look like most of the rooms in which Quaker silence is practiced it would be bare and beige. No crosses, flags, banners, icons, or anything else even remotely religious-looking adorn traditional Quaker meeting rooms. Though you might find such things helpful for practicing your silence, Friends focus on simplicity, feeling that the presence of open, worshipful hearts and God's spirit make a place holy.

So create a space that speaks to *your* soul's condition. It could be a corner of the bedroom, with an easy chair and soft light, like it was for me. It could be a larger space, with a table and a meditation candle. It can be inside, or outside.

For my wife, Nancy, it's often outside. If we're seaside, Nancy revels in the sacrament of sand—time alone with God early in the morning on the shore. Nancy practices soulful silence as she walks early in the day, watching seabirds and picking up shells, with the salt-air tousling her hair. She revels in God's creation—the new sun and the timeless tide. She carves out spaces where God can speak clearly to her. I'm invited into those times back at the condo when I see the radiance of her face.

The important thing is not *where*—it is where *for you?* Nancy's places are not mine. Mine are not hers. Hers would drive me to distraction. I like flowers and plants, but only to look at, not to be quiet in. God could speak to me there, but I know I'm more intentionally quiet in my study. I'm more able to hear God there than in the garden. If Nancy were in my study, though, she'd be looking at all the books and pulling them down and trying to figure out which one to read. God would be there with tapping foot and clearing throat to get her attention—if God were that way. Which, thankfully, God is not. God is loving and patient and kind (as well as fiercely holy) and willingly meets us where we can best converse. That conversation is a gift of Quaker silence.

Quietude Query

⬎ Relax your body and mind.

⬎ Breathe deeply.

⬎ Put down the book.

⬎ Think about the following Quietude Query slowly and gently. Savor each thought.

⬎ Think of my sacred silent space. What would it look like? How would I furnish it?

While one of the strengths of Quaker silence is that it requires no special time, in the beginning (and sometimes throughout our entire lives, depending on our personalities) it can be helpful to set aside specific times for silence. Otherwise we may find the affairs of the day so overtaking us that we don't have time to be quiet until we go to bed. Then we promptly fall asleep. That's not to say God can't speak to us in the silence of our dreams. There are plenty of biblical examples of God doing just that. But sleepy spirituality certainly robs us of the joy of dialogue. It steals the sensuality of the divine encounter.

Pierre Lacout captured that sensuality when he wrote, "In silence which is active, the Inner Light begins to glow—a tiny spark. For the flame to be kindled and to grow, subtle argument and the clamor of our emotions must be stilled. It is by an attention full of love that we enable the Inner Light to blaze and illuminate our dwelling and to make of our whole being a source from which this Light may shine out. Words must be purified in a redemptive silence if they are to bear the message of peace. The right to speak is a call to the duty of listening. Speech has no meaning unless there are attentive minds and silent hearts. Silence is the welcoming acceptance of the other. The word born of silence must be received in silence."

For the purpose of being alone and still before God, you might want to make a regular, non-negotiable place in your schedule. Maybe that's early in the morning for you. It wouldn't be for me. I hate getting up. But Nancy loves it. At home, when possible, she practices garden silence—sweet communion with God's growing things. That's because all of creation continually reminds her of the goodness and love of God. As Sharron Singleton writes in her poem *All the News:*

> Some look to angels
> for news of the holy.
> on my knees in the earth
> of my garden,
> hot sun rakes
> my hair, licks

> my neck, presses
> me down, stuns
> me with all the news
> I can bear.

Finding time for holy silence isn't something that is added to our "To Do" list. To spend time with the One who loves us so dearly should not be a chore to be checked off, but something our heart desires, something our soul longs for. More like a "Want To Do" list. If we are serious about seeking God, that is. Thomas Kelly asks a hard question— "Do you *want* to live in such an amazing divine Presence that life is transformed and transfigured and transmuted into peace and power and glory and miracle?" If we can honestly answer, "Yes," then Kelly's response is, "If you do, you can. But if you say you haven't the time to go down into the recreating silences, I can only say to you, 'Then you don't really want to. . . . For . . . we find time for what we *really want* to do.'"

While Kelly's words may seem a bit harsh, even parental, they're not meant that way. He asks that we be honest about our intentions. At writing conferences I often meet sincere people who tell me, "I'd like to write a book." I smile, because I know what's coming next. "But I just don't have the time," they say. I wouldn't have the time either, except that writing is something I love and feel compelled to do. It's the same way with what Kelly is saying—if we honestly answer "Yes" then we'll find time, because we always find time, no matter how pressured we are, for the things and people that matter to us.

Notice that Kelly doesn't say how much time is the "right" amount of time. He is not very concerned with the quantity. It's the quality and intention of coming to God in silence. Silence isn't an added religious duty. Holy silence is not one more thing to do. It is something we do that gives us, in a strange way, more time. It doesn't take time away. Holy silence is like love in that way. We can have love and give love and still have an abundant store. There is nothing to fear in giving away love.

Likewise, the time we devote to the miracle of the mysterious encounter with Christ in stillness comes back to us. I don't mean that minutes are physically put back on the clock or that the sun stands still in its orbit. No, what I mean is that our rushing slows, our thoughts clear, our priorities reorder themselves. When we are silent we are issued into that divine presence that ordered the universe and helps us order our lives in ways that bring serenity and a seeming enlargement of both our energy and our day.

Quietude Query

🖎 Relax your body and mind.

🖎 Breathe deeply.

🖎 Put down the book.

🖎 Think about the following Quietude Query slowly and gently. Savor each thought.

🖎 How could taking time for silence enlarge my day?

Of course it isn't absolutely necessary to get far away from noises and people to hear God speak. If that were the case then we would rarely perceive God's promptings. But we may find it's best to eliminate the voices of the world so that we can hear God's voice undistracted. As King David says in the Psalms, "For God alone my soul waits in silence; . . . For God alone my soul waits in silence, for my hope is from him."

Quaker silence also allows for spontaneous encounters with God. Though you may set aside certain times for silence, holy silence can be practiced at any time. You may wish to take time for silence by leaving the television and radio off and simply holding silence lightly. I don't recommend practicing spiritual silence while driving, though. For me, being silent means focusing a certain level of my attention on being still. That means my outward activity tends to slow. This is super annoying to the other drivers—not to mention dangerous. A paraphrase of the words of the narrator on my fear of flying self-hypnosis CD applies here—"Under no circumstances should you attempt silence whilst driving an automobile."

So how do you begin the practice of holding silence? One way to begin is to start by either sitting or lying down; whichever is more comfortable and appropriate. *Appropriate* is a key word. You probably don't want to stretch out on top of your desk at work.

Then close your eyes and take a deep breath. Really deep. Inhale and exhale slowly. Then do it even more slowly. It will seem forced at first. It will, however, help you become aware of breathing, and the tenseness surrounding your body and soul. Let your breath go down through your chest and into your every cell. Feel your body gently rise and fall as you inhale and exhale.

As you breathe, listen for the voice of the Spirit. Even listen for your own voice. What are you saying to you? What is God saying? Don't expect to hear or sense something immediately. This isn't something that happens after one or two breaths. It's not like, "Well, I've breathed five times and nothing's happened yet, so I guess I'll go mow the lawn." Relax into relaxing. Relax into silence.

If you're having a hard time focusing on the silence, you might want to use a word or verse of Scripture or a prayer. Think about the various names given to Jesus— Emmanuel, the Word, the Light, Prince of Peace, Morning Star, and the Good Shepherd. For many of us, the first steps we take into the world of silence are through the words of prayer. I use the Lord's Prayer, both the traditional version and a contemporary musical version by John Fischer.

> Holy Father hear our prayer.
> Keep us always in Your care.
> May Your kingdom come to us
> And may we learn how to trust.
> Do Your will among us now
> As we here before You bow.
> Give to us but what we need

As upon Your word we feed.

Keep us from the things that do You wrong

When we're weak because we think we're strong.

Save us from our selfish desire.

Fill us and with Your love inspire.

Honor, greatness belong to You

Love and peace and mercy, too

Praise to You again and again. Amen.

I hum the tune in my head and my heart sings the lyrics. You may want to sing, recite Scripture, remember something you've read, or call to mind some special spiritual words or phrases. All of these—and any others you come up with—are okay. Remember, Quakers have no rulebook. Use these as tools to help you focus on the eternal rather than the external.

When you first begin practicing silence you might find it hard to stay focused. Your thoughts may wander. That's okay. The way of silence is not easy. It's reported that Abbot Agatho, one of those crazy holy desert fathers, carried a stone in his mouth for three years "until he learned to be silent." That's a rather discomfiting image—but one that is also reassuring. If a monastic father takes three years to learn to be silent, you don't have to expect to be able to learn it in three easy steps. Nothing worth doing seems to be achieved quickly—gardening, writing, or tending the soul. "The mind wanders and the will falters again and again," writes Thomas Green. ". . . But it is foolish to allow failures in concentration 'to plunge us into profitless self-condemnation'. . . . God is similarly pleased with our efforts and understanding of our many failures." God will meet you in the effort. Don't get discouraged if your thoughts turn from the deep stuff of the Spirit to that ugly crack in the ceiling that you've been meaning to fix. Don't worry about it. The crack in the ceiling is part of your life, too. It is fine to be present where you are.

When the crack, or other distractions, begin bothering you, bring yourself back to your breath. The more you practice, the easier it gets—the more relaxed you become. Settle briefly and silently. Think again about sacred words, prayers, songs, or Scripture. Use them as signs to God that you are ready to encounter the eternal. See them as a way of becoming open to God's words and presence. Silence is a way to reconnect, in love, with God.

Quietude Query

🥀 Relax your body and mind.

🥀 Breathe deeply.

🥀 Put down the book.

🥀 Think about the following Quietude Query slowly and gently. Savor each thought.

🥀 What sacred words or prayers or songs would I use to help center into the silence?

If we think about the Eucharist, the Lord's Supper, as the great central act of liturgical Christian worship, we see that it works at many levels and is explained theologically in a variety of ways depending upon one's denominational slant. Every Christian tradition has its own theology to explain the meaning of the Eucharist. One tradition agrees in places with other traditions, and disagrees in others. Sometimes we describe seemingly identical concepts with very different words. Every Christian—even Quakers who don't use bread and wine—agree that the Lord's Supper is an enactment of a divine mystery. It is a paradox, like a great deal of Christian faith.

The Lord's Supper uses the earthly elements of bread and wine to tell truth about God. As a liturgical act it take in many matters—a longing to be with God and to live a life faithful to God and family, feeling sorry about shortcomings, being grateful for life's God-given goodness, and tendered by love for all of God's creatures. The Eucharist announces an eternal "ally-ally in free," and at the same time it says, "You're it"—the real game of life continues. The Eucharist anchors Christians securely in the world and enables us to live well in it through our taking Jesus into our selves.

It does all these things because in the Eucharist liturgical Christians expect to encounter the real presence of Christ. Think of Jesus standing with us. Could we stand next to holy, loving Jesus and not seek salvation and reconciliation? Could anyone feed on Him in her heart and not feel strengthened? Jesus' presence with us humbles, empowers, and lifts us.

When we participate in holy silence, all of these dimensions of the Eucharistic feast come into play. It differs significantly from the outward forms in that there is no physical bread or wine and that holy silence can be held at any time. The presence of Christ is open to us at all times through the spiritual practice of holy silence.

Tony Hendra in his book *Father Joe: The Man Who Saved My Soul,* talks about the sanctuary lamp hanging near the tabernacle of consecrated wafers in a Catholic church as honoring and indicating that Christ is present. "The Savior is . . . IN," he gently jokes. In Quaker silence the Savior is always in . . . and available to feed us. We become the liturgist, priest, penitent, and communicant.

The Eucharist and Quaker silence are both mysteries of Christian faith and practice. There are various theological theories about how the Eucharist works (transubstantiation, consubstantiation, *et al*). But those who experience Christ in their hearts and souls worry less about the "how" or the "why," than being happy that it "is." The same is true of Quaker silence. In my younger life I sold fax machines when they were new on the market. As a salesperson, not an engineer, I couldn't answer the most common question people asked me— "How does it work?" How can a plastic box filled with electronics hook into a phone line and then produce a piece of paper full of words that looks exactly like a piece of paper full of words that is physically half a world away? Lacking a technological explanation, I used to answer, "It's magic." While what happens in the Eucharist is not technology or magic, it certainly is mysterious. Everything about God is. That is, in some ways, what I am saying about the Eucharistic nature of Quaker silence. How can it be that by sitting in silence a worshiper is joined with the real presence of Christ? Theological musings and explanations have their time and place. These explanations inevitably fall short, however. Who can know the mind of God? Who can explain God's ways? Theological musing is interesting, but often un-understandable to the average person. That is okay, though, because most average people of faith don't want to know *how*—we just want to know *God*. We want to enjoy God's presence in and through and around us. That is what holy silence invites us to do.

Quietude Query

∽ Relax your body and mind.

∽ Breathe deeply.

∽ Put down the book.

∽ Think about the following Quietude Query slowly and gently. Savor each thought.

∽ What do I feel that indicates God's presence with me?

That noisy television night—after excusing myself from the din and making my way upstairs, I settled in the chair and turned the bedside lamp on low. I began paying attention to my breathing. Slow. Slower. Slower. Pieces of noise fell away. The television soundtrack receded. We had the windows open in the non-air-conditioned house. A light breeze tossed the curtains gently. Floating on the soft wind came the early summer sounds of cicadas and frogs in the pond. Good sounds. Natural sounds. God-made sounds. I picked up a book of poems by the nineteenth-century Quaker poet John Greenleaf Whittier. Leafing through it, I came across these lines from "Revelation":

> I pray for faith, I long to trust;
> I listen with my heart, and hear
> A Voice without a sound: "Be just,
> Be true, be merciful, revere
> The Word within thee: God is near!"

> I fear no more. The clouded face
> Of Nature smiles; through all her things
> Of time and space and sense I trace
> The moving of the Spirit's wings,
> And hear the song of hope she sings.

As peace filled me I remembered that there is no secret to achieving silence other than just doing it. Be quiet. In the silence of a hastily prepared heart and mind I met God—the great Lover of my soul.

CHAPTER FIVE

Gathering
Practicing Communal Silence

Quakers don't usually go to Mass. But ten of us did one Saturday night. We went as one of the spiritual field trips Nancy and I organized to help young Friends in Muncie understand and appreciate the diversity of religious experience and their own Friendly heritage. Each week we visited a church different from ours or invited someone from another faith tradition to come speak to us. The final night of the series found us at St. Francis of Assisi Church.

Father Michael McKinney and I had become friends, mostly through serving on panels about religion at various gatherings around the Ball State University campus. Father Mike and I, though miles apart liturgically, often ended up in about the same place theologically and sacramentally. Both of us believed in the power of the sacraments. We just disagreed about their number and form. When I told him I'd like to bring our group to Mass, he was very welcoming. Father Mike met us before the service to explain a bit of what would happen. The kids were Quakers and didn't have a clear idea of the liturgy of Mass.

Since it was a Saturday night Mass, it didn't have all the "smells and bells," as some of my Catholic friends call them. Still, it was impressive to a bunch of people who aren't used to robed clergy, candles, crosses, or stained glass windows. The kids, and Nancy and I, were enthralled and moved, especially when the Sacred Host was elevated during the consecration.

Later when we all went out to eat (Quakers think everything religious is better when food is involved), I asked, "So, what does silence in Quaker meeting correspond to in the Catholic Mass?" "The music," offered one kid, hopefully. "The sermon (homily)?" asked another. They stopped guessing and thought awhile. "I know," said one of them. "The Eucharist." "Yeah," added another, "that was when we really felt like Jesus was there." "It got so quiet," someone else said. "So, you mean silence is our sacrament?" I asked. They nodded and smiled. The light—and the Light—had finally dawned on them. Silence is where Quakers believe we encounter the real presence of Christ. Since we don't have rites or symbols, or use bread or wine, Jesus comes to us in the peace of the silence. That night I felt like our young Friends finally and truly understood the importance of Quaker silence and its Eucharistic nature.

Silence, when we worship with others, becomes a means of grace. That's because it brings us into God's presence. Worship becomes Eucharistic when we sense God present with our group. Some English Friends said, "In a meeting for worship Friends gather in silence as a congregation of seeking souls, and as they unite together in worship there comes a spiritual harmony." This spiritual harmony occurs first among those who gather. Then it grows between them and the Spirit of God. Yes, we can worship alone. There are times in our private spiritual silences that our hearts break in silent adoration from the presence of the eternal in our lives. When we join others in silent, expectant waiting, though, it is probable that we will discover a deeper sense of God's presence in our lives individually and corporately than we could in solitary contemplation. It is as if we were each candles. Each gives off a little light where it is. But when the candles are brought together and placed on the altar of worship, then the entire holy space is bathed in warm, flickering light. Communal, silent worship is a way of sharing our light with each other and with God.

Communal Quaker worship is more than people getting together to pray quietly, solitarily, in the same place. Beatrice Saxon Snell compared it to the difference between a symphony and a solo: ". . . those who persevere in group worship know that it differs from private devotion as the music of an orchestra differs from the music of a single player." Corporate Quaker worship is not a time of individual meditation. Communal silence is not a time to relax or gather one's thoughts. It is important that the waiting and the listening in silence are done as a group. The people who gather, do so with the hope of becoming something more than just a collection of individuals meeting in the same room. They have gathered to be part of the body of Christ on earth. In silent, communal worship we remain individuals—just like the instruments in an orchestra are not blended into one giant tuba or violin, but remain distinct. Like an orchestra, we have a director leading us in one song—in this case a spiritual one.

Quietude Query

෴ Relax your body and mind.

෴ Breathe deeply.

෴ Put down the book.

෴ Think about the following Quietude Query slowly and gently. Savor each thought.

෴ What group—existing or new—could I hold silence with?

An observer coming into silent meeting may think that it just looks like a bunch of people sitting silently in rows next to, but not connected to one another. He'd be wrong. Yes, much of what we do is personal. But in this group silence we come as seekers of the spirit, individuals united in and by our spiritual goal—to experience God. In that way it's similar to other

Christian worship services. When I attend North United Methodist Church to hear my friend Kevin preach, I am there with six hundred other folks. Like them I'm listening as an individual, but we hear jointly. When my friend Sue attends Mass at Saint Joan of Arc, she receives Holy Communion personally, but joins the other worshipers in doing so collectively. It's that same way in Quaker silence. We are personally silent while we are silent communally.

This gathered worship, as Quakers call it, is not only absence of noise. Gathered worship springs from the reverent, silent expectation that God will come among the people. The silence deepens as we feel ourselves drawn beautifully to God and each other. Our hearts and souls burst with thanksgiving—a thanksgiving best expressed by silence. Silence growing from awe is the natural human response to hints of the Divine. An audience is often struck silent after an especially moving piece of music, because it recognizes intimations of the eternal in the music, even if the group can't name the piece.

While Quaker worship doesn't appear to follow a set liturgy or code of rules, and a silent service has no set structure, it's a bit more complicated than that. Yes, Quakers do without an outward liturgy. But that doesn't mean that liturgy is absent. Let's take a look at "liturgy." (This is the point where my kids sigh and say, "Yes, Mr. Word-person.") We get our modern day "liturgy" from the Latin *liturgia*, which comes from the Greek *leitourgia*.

Leitourgia means "public service of God." Today's word of course has grown to mean a ritual for public worship, one that uses prescribed forms.

Quaker worship has always been a public service of God. And it does use a prescribed form—it's just that, since it is silent, it's not perceived as such. What "silent liturgy" does is make communal worship quickly participatory. From the time we settle into our seats, everybody gathered has a part—not just a preacher preaching, a choir choiring, or an organist organizing. It is an unrecognized liturgy that involves everyone. Robert Lawrence Smith in his little book, *A Quaker Book of Wisdom* says, "I have always felt that . . . there was, and still is, something . . . profoundly democratic about this optimistic faith that declares that all people are created equal; . . . that insists on the freedom to worship in whatever form one chooses—and that recognizes a direct one-to-one relationship with God." It's that "democratic" nature that "recognizes a direct one-to-one relationship with God" and "that all people are created equal" that makes Quaker silence a participatory liturgy.

In the same way that no written liturgy is used for Quaker worship, neither is there formal sacred space. To a Quaker all space is sacred space, though one of the most surprising places Quaker silence was ever held was Gestapo headquarters. Rufus Jones, George Walton, and Robert Yarnall went to Germany to find out how Quakers could help the Jews. Their trip came shortly after *Kristallnacht* in November 1938. After their arrival in Berlin, it soon became evident that they would have to have any action approved by Reinhard Heydrich of the Gestapo. Heydrich wanted them flustered and so had two of his underlings keep the Quakers cooling their heels in the lobby of Gestapo headquarters. Instead of being upset, they held silent meeting. "During this awesome period," reports Jones, "we bowed our heads and entered upon a time of deep, quiet meditation and prayer. . . . It proved to be rightly ordered. The two men returned at the announced time and the leader said, 'Everything you have asked for is granted.'"

What these three wise men (as Josef Goebbels called them) did is not unusual. Quakers have worshiped in lots of places. Early Quaker meetings often convened in fields, barns, pubs, and homes. That democracy of space continues today. All that matters is that two or more come together with a hunger for the presence of God. The way of Quaker silence is open to anyone or any group who wants to experience God in a new way. As with any faith tradition, it is the intention to worship that makes a time and place holy.

So, what happens in Quaker worship? Peeking in the Meetinghouse window, you would think, *not much*. It's quiet, after all. But a lot is happening. You just can't see it.

Many Friends settle into silence by reflecting on the old Quaker saying, "Turn in thy mind to the Light, and wait upon God." That adage helps us remember why we're gathering in silence. We want our minds turned to the light of Christ. We are there to wait upon God. In this way, waiting for God is similar to Samuel Beckett's *Waiting for Godot*. The two tramps waiting for the arrival of M. Godot don't just sit there and wait. All sorts of stuff is going on with them—they fuss, make up, try to sleep, eat, and contemplate the great themes of life. The same is often true of our communal silent waiting for God.

Quietude Query

⮑ Relax your body and mind.

⮑ Breathe deeply.

⮑ Put down the book.

⮑ Think about the following Quietude Query slowly and gently. Savor each thought.

⮑ Can I imagine silence being active for a group of people I love and feel called to worship with?

It's active, too, because the ministry of silence requires participation by every person present. Then, together, as we engage the depths of living silence, we are more than just waiting for God—we encounter God. We also encounter each other in stillness in a way that we don't in the everyday world of "Hi, how are you" and other rhetorical niceties. Sitting in silence, we notice the folks around us. As we see their heads bowed or their eyes looking toward heaven, we wonder, *How are they?*

And then we remember a snippet of something said about school or a sick parent or a job promotion. We pray for them. They, in the silence, settle into our soul and join us. At the same time that we hold them in God's light, they hold us. Our wondering about whether we set the timer on the oven or how the trustees could ever have picked mauve carpeting passes away as we come into the light of God. In that light, we feel ourselves drawn to each other and God.

One thing that surprises many first-time visitors to Quaker worship is that people speak. That's something else that sets Quaker communal worship apart from a private devotional life of silence. The thought that spoken words are a part of communal silent worship sounds odd. But this speaking comes from more than a mere urge to say something. In Quaker meeting, a person speaks only if convinced that something must be shared. My friend Canby always told me, "Speak only if you can improve the silence."

Generally, if someone is led to speak, her words are brief. They could include readings from the Bible or other books, praying, singing, or speaking from personal experience—a mini-sermonette, if you will. The words need to come from the speaker's soul, rather than the mind. As Nancy always reminds me, "Speak from the heart, not the head."

That's not to downplay the intellect. But discussion and argument—even of a theological nature—have no part in silent worship. Neither do business keeping announcements. Worship is not discussion or reporting time. Being dazzled by a speaker's brilliance, or hearing that there's a Chevy with its lights on in the parking lot, is not the point of Quaker silent worship. The point is hearing God.

Sometimes, we forget that. Especially those of us who like the sound of our voices and our brainpower. Rufus Jones once told a joke on himself about speaking in meeting after he came home from college. After his brilliant sermon, and the appropriate silence, another Friend stood and admonished, "Jesus said, 'Feed my sheep,' not 'Feed my giraffes.'" Rufus got the point. What he said was deep—or in this case, high over the listeners' heads. He spoke to impress, not express the love of God. We hear God best in words that spring from a speaker's heart and soul.

Another of the democratic principles of Quaker silence is that anyone may speak as led by God's spirit. Everyone present, even a child, is encouraged to take an active part in Meeting by speaking.

For those of us adults who know that kids say some crazy things, this can be a little frightening. Still, young souls sometimes display more sensitivity to the Spirit than some of us older, more spiritually cynical folks. If you tell a child to listen and see what God has to say, she will. Some kids can be quite good in delivering God's message to us in ways that we truly hear it—freshly, spontaneously, unpompously. Some friends of ours had a young son whom they took to Quaker worship. They explained Quaker liturgy—sit silent, very silent, listen for God, and if led, then speak. "Kids, too?" he asked.

"Kids, too," they answered nervously.

After everyone settled in the quiet room, silence settled over the Friends like a warm blanket, cozy in God's comfort. Lance began to stir. "God's telling me to talk."

"Make sure," said his dad, planting his elbow and upper arm firmly against the boy's body snuggled against him.

"I'm sure," Lance said. But his dad's arm didn't move. When the pressure eased from Burt's need to change positions, Lance shot up, as did his parent's eyebrows and blood pressure. "I hear God talking to me through the clock. The clock says, 'Tick . . . tock . . . tick . . . tock . . . don't waste . . . God's time . . . don't waste . . . God's time." Then he sat down.

His speaking met Canby's test. Lance improved the silence.

Friends believe that God speaks through the vocal contributions made at the meeting—and the silence. That's why each sharing is followed by a period of silence. The silence lets us reflect on what God has said through the words shared. It gives our hearts time to hear the message. Our brains may have heard it right away, but our hearts often take longer. Words that linger in our hearts are often more helpful than those that pass quickly through our brains.

When the words come from God, so too does a feeling as if a divine presence has settled over the group. That feeling is a conscientious response to a speaker's carefully discerned leading of the Spirit. Our souls recognize words that come from a place beyond intellect. In the eighteenth century, John Woolman made a difficult and dangerous trip into Indian country. He remained at an Indian camp for four days, preaching, worshiping, and praying with the Indians. Once, during his time there, he forgot about the interpreters and poured out his heart in prayer, in English. Instead of being confused by what Woolman had said in his foreign tongue, the Indian chief Papunehang put his hand on his own breast and declared, "I love to feel where the words come from."

Some of the best sermons are those least polished or grammatically correct. Don't worry if you failed public speaking. As God showed Moses, faltering and stuttering are fine—it's not the messenger: it's the message.

Quietude Query

⟜ Relax your body and mind.

⟜ Breathe deeply.

⟜ Put down the book.

⟜ Think about the following Quietude Query slowly and gently. Savor each thought.

⟜ How would I know when I am being led to break the silence?

Of course that really gets tested if the person speaking is someone we don't particularly care for or we find annoying. As one Friend prayed, when he heard that a visiting minister whom he didn't like was attending worship that day, "Oh Lord, thou knowest that we are about to hear a great many things that are not true." J. Ormerod Greenwood, an English Friend, once wrote, ". . . In my young tempestuous days I heard many things in the Friends' meeting that I disliked and some that seemed to me quite false, and I felt the need to answer them." Someone may indeed say something, or many things, that we disagree with. Our natural inclination is to jump up and say something like, "The way that Friend put it was a way that would not have occurred to me," which is Quaker-ese for "Can you believe that craziness? Now get ready for the straight dope." But Greenwood has a lesson for us. His writing continues, "I was taught, and I believe correctly, that to insist on answering there and then would be to destroy the meeting; and that we all sit under the baptising power of the spirit of Truth, which is its own witness. We sit in silence so as not to trip over words; and we trust the good in each other which is from God, so that we may be kept from the evil."

The old adage that "God moves in mysterious ways" can be rephrased in Quaker-ese to "God speaks through mysterious speakers." That's why two themes run through Quaker meeting—waiting and listening. We wait to feel the touch of the Divine, and we listen too for God's voice in both the silence and the speakers.

Let the silence continue until someone is led by the Spirit of God to speak. Don't worry if no one says anything. It's okay for a meeting to be completely silent. If God is there, and everyone is actively engaged in worship, it will be a meeting of peace, depth, and unity regardless of whether there is vocal ministry or not. Completely silent worship can be refreshing and strengthening. It provides space to get away from all the stuff that presses in on us—office work, home work, yard work. It takes us to a place where we feel closer to God and each other. The holy silence itself is worship.

Another thing that happens in communal silence is that God gives us power to help us live as we should, and want, to live. William Penn once wrote, "True godliness does not turn men out of the world, but enables them to live better in it and excites their endeavors to mend it." While the wording is a bit archaic, the sentiment isn't. The shared silence gives us strength to live well in the world. That's why there is no such thing as a Quaker hermit. As Robert Barclay wrote, "When I came into the silent assemblies of God's people, I felt a secret power among them, which touched my heart; and as I gave way unto it I found the evil weakening in me and the good raised up; and so I became thus knit and united unto them, hungering more and more after the increase of this power and life whereby I might feel myself perfectly redeemed; and indeed this is the surest way to become a Christian."

The silence calls us to ask, "What does God want?" instead of our usual "What do I want?" In silence what God wants becomes clear. I know I should be more patient with people, especially Nancy. She's always late. That drives me crazy. In the silence of Meeting, though, I feel my irritation fade as it becomes clear to me that what God wants is for me to love Nancy—not make sure we're on time to church. As I think about being more patient, I know that I need to begin by apologizing to her. So, in the silence, I reach for her hand. Words can come later. It is in the silence of the gathered Meeting that this becomes clear to me—not in the frosty silence rushing to the Meetinghouse. God's direction comes, in part, because I want to know what God wants from me. So God reveals it. That's the promise Jesus gave in the Gospels: "Ask, and it will be given you; seek, and you will find; knock, and it will be opened to you. For every one who asks receives, and he who seeks finds, and to him who knocks it will be opened." If we ask, seek, and knock in the silence, God makes the divine will known to us.

Experiential is a major vocabulary word for Friends, especially as it relates to matters of faith and worship. One of the effects we experience in communal silent worship is feeling surrounded by the people and God we love. Of course, we may also be angry with someone who's at worship. We are, after all, just people—messed-up, blessed human beings trying however badly to make our way to loving God and loving each other. Sometimes, though, we'd like to leave that last part out. It's easy to love God; God's not sitting next to us needing a shower or stronger deodorant. It's harder to love that annoyingly human being in the next chair that needs both. This means that we need to start with forgiveness—of them and us. If we can forgive the alto who's always off-key or the greeter who didn't seem very friendly when we came in, and if we can forgive ourselves for being irked by these two, and if we can hold them in God's light, then we find silence erasing our separateness and blending us into Christ's body in this place. When we reach that point, we sense that we are part of God's family. We see that these are our brothers and sisters around us. Yes, this family can be dysfunctional, but when God is there it becomes a family of mutual love and support. To feel such love and support is worth an hour of silence a week.

Quietude Query

☙ Relax your body and mind.

☙ Breathe deeply.

☙ Put down the book.

☙ Think about the following Quietude Query slowly and gently. Savor each thought.

☙ What could a communal experience of God feel like?

Since every Friends Meeting for Worship is experiential, it is also an experiment. There are no guarantees that God's presence will be felt. Worship based on silence has no creed, no sacraments, and no presiding ministers to help it along. Instead, we gather to nurture each other in love by sharing silence, Scriptures, sorrows, *leadings*, prayers, and hopes. It is not a passive silence, but an active going toward God, seeking a glimpse of the Divine. The special discipline we Quakers practice is listening with more than our ears. We listen for the Voice that speaks not only in words, but also in gentle tugs on our hearts and in the beauty our eyes behold.

So, how do you plan Quaker worship? First, find a place. Again, it's not important where the place is. Arrange the room so that participants face each other in a square or a circle. This keeps folks aware that they are a group gathered for worship—not just people who happen to be sitting in the same room. One of the positives about this arrangement is that it also reminds us that we are all on equal footing before each other and God.

Next . . . well, there is no next—other than inviting people to join in worship. You don't have to gather any prayer books, hymnals, liturgies, or on-line sermons. All you need to do is set the time and place.

Don't expect to sit still for an hour and have godly thoughts every moment. If you're human that is.

Planning a Quaker worship service for your friends or church group is easy enough. Well, easy other than scaring them with the idea of having to sit silently for an hour. Especially if they've never done it before.

Ease their fears by letting them know what to expect and how they can prepare for silence. I wish someone had clued me in the first time I went to Mass as a Quaker kid. The Mass was a wedding and it was pre-Vatican II. Nobody told me what to expect. I walked into the church and immediately plopped down the really cool footrests. My parents were appalled. They quickly brushed my feet off the kneeler and put it back into place. Then we stood up and sat down and people chanted in a weird language. "It's Latin," my dad whispered. Their preacher—I found out later he was called a priest—was decked out like it was Halloween. After I got used to it, it was cool in a strange sort of way. Still, I wished somebody had told me what to expect.

Folks who are used to structure in worship—whether high church or Pentecostal or of another faith tradition altogether—may find it helpful to think of Quaker worship, even if it is silence, as having structure. You might even want to print a short summary of what's going to happen—an order of worship for a non-ordered worship. The basic elements are Centering, Welcoming, Deep Worship, Communion, and Sending.

All silent meetings begin with centering. That's when the service starts and worshipers begin growing silent. It's a time to acknowledge in the silence that you're carrying lots of concerns with you, like work, school, family. It's also the time to say, *I'm going to set these aside during this worship time.* This does not deny the kids' problems, outside noises, health, pain, disagreements, conflict, or future responsibilities. Let them all bubble to the surface in this centering time.

Then wash them away in the river of God's love. Don't be surprised when, just like an artesian well, your worries, sadness, joy, and hopes flow freshly to the surface. Don't worry if they do. Just let them flow and go. If they return during meeting for worship, send them down river before they have the chance to dam the spiritual stream and bring the fresh water of God to a halt.

Sometimes, of course, our thoughts are not personal. They don't have anything to do with worrying whether or not we left the coffeemaker on or locked the back door. Issues like peace in the Middle East seem to be more worthy of God's attention. We think, *How will God know they are on our hearts if we don't say something?* We're like the old Quaker who stood up in Meeting and prayed, "Oh God, as you undoubtedly read in *The Guardian.* . . ." We want to make sure God knows what's going on. Still, even these "big" issues need to be dismissed. Leaving them unspoken, we hand them over to God and trust that God will care for them.

If thoughts keep popping up, don't fight them. Don't try to bash them into silence by sheer force of will. Embrace silent worship as the chance to escape from them. Turn from them to the motivation for gathering together—to meet Jesus. Then slowly the thoughts of everyday living will ebb. You'll find yourself ready to meet God. As Rachel Needham wrote, "Value the opportunity to think unguided by the world. Learn what you feel you need to know, let other information pass. No moment of silence is a waste of time."

It goes against our grain to sit and "do nothing." We don't want to waste time. But sometimes we fear the silence. Noise helps us block out self-searching and soul-searching thoughts. It keeps us from being vulnerable—or at least feeling vulnerable. Intellectually we may know that we can't hide from God. But we also know it's harder to hear God's voice—loving or corrective—when we're surrounded by sound. Being surrounded by spiritual silence and the company of other souls opens us up to meeting God. This can be both peace-giving and terrifying. What if His word is not one of comfort, but of command? That's what always used to scare me. What if I get silent and I hear, "Brent, go to Africa"? I don't like leaving the Midwest and I hate flying—so Africa terrifies me. I'd sing the missionary chorus, "I'll go where you want me to go, dear Lord," silently adding, "as long as it's in Ohio."

Yes, God may speak a command in the silence. But remember that God wants our fellowship. God is not looking to slap us down or around. We do a pretty good job of that ourselves. When we get quiet and still together, we create a space for God to work within us personally and communally. We give ourselves a chance to rest and let that perfect love which drives out fear do its work. Don't rush your centering time. If you've allowed an hour for worship, don't be dismayed if it takes ten minutes to empty your mind of the day's concerns. You'd wait longer than that to ride Space Mountain at Disney World—and not receive half the benefit.

Next, welcome God. That's not to say that God wasn't already there. It's more like the purpose of an invocation at the start of a liturgical service. It is time to acknowledge God's presence in the room, and in your soul. Relax into the love of God surrounding you. Acknowledge the others in the room. It's okay to look around at God's gathered people. You may want to pray for each one, bringing their needs, known and unknown to you, to God. Welcoming is a time for gratitude for other people's love and care. Welcome and thankfulness walk hand in hand here, in deep, respectful silence. It is a blessing to worship with the family of God.

During most of the rest of our lives—while we *know* that we are part of a people trying to be God's hands, feet, eyes, and ears on earth—we may not *feel* it. Silent worship lets us focus on the people whom God has called together for this hour. They may not, at least on the surface, be the people we would have chosen. God's ways are not our ways, though, and for some inscrutable, eternal reason God has decided that even the most annoying among us are precious in His sight. They need to be so in ours, as well. So in silence, allow the folks *sitting* close to you to *draw spiritually* close to you. They are your family in faith and worship. Remember them in your heart. They've come bringing some of the same worries about family and work and the world you've brought—as well as their own particular joys and sorrows. This is an opportunity to look for that of God in each person—even the annoying ones. God, in silent working, can turn these annoyances into blessings. Michael Birkel reminds us that, "What otherwise would be distractions can be woven into a prayerful frame of mind. A baby's babbling moves one to joy and gratitude for newness of life. A neighbor's coughing inspires a prayer for her health. Gladly received, such sounds lose their potential to distract, so the task is to cultivate a disposition of grateful receptivity."

Quietude Query

⬧ Relax your body and mind.

⬧ Breathe deeply.

⬧ Put down the book.

⬧ Think about the following Quietude Query slowly and gently. Savor each thought.

⬧ Who among those that I worship with could use a prayer out of my silence right now?

Now it is time to move on to deep silent worship. You've cast off from the shores and made your way cautiously around the edge of the spiritual sea. Now it is time to launch out to the depths. We live so much of life on the surface—hardly ever dipping below the surface of either our cares or our joys. We rarely examine why we are happy or sad. We accept happiness as something we're due and medicate any sorrow. We often avoid looking at the reasons behind our feelings. This portion of silent worship, though, calls us to a place that is both emotionally higher and spiritually deeper than any place we normally live in. It takes us to a place where, safe in God and with our friends, we move inside our souls, a spiritual flashlight in our hands, peering across the ocean of life. As we go, God goes with us. Jesus moves across the waves, calling to the waves in our lives, "Peace, be still." And our tiny spiritual flashlight fades as His searchlight illuminates the ocean in front of, around, and behind us.

As this happens, you may find Scripture passages or hymns on the themes of awe, gratitude, and praise welling up inside you. Let them come. Release them in your soul. Let your voice speak them, if necessary. God's love is even wider and deeper than the sea you've launched out on. God's love carries us over the troubled waters of life and brings us to a true sea of tranquility. George Fox once wrote, "I saw, also, that there was an ocean of darkness and death; but an infinite ocean of light and love, which flowed over the ocean of darkness. In that also I saw the infinite love of God." Silent worship leads us onto that infinite ocean of light where the waves are still.

Even here, in the still waters of the soul, you might find it helpful to focus on images of Jesus—Living Stone, Bread of Life, Head of the Church, and other biblical names. Images focus the mind, so that our soul's eyes gaze upon God in simple, loving openness. Or you might want to think about various Bible characters—Ruth, David, Timothy, Mary, and Barnabas. How do you see God at work in these folks? Do you know these people of faith? Imagining yourself in their places can help you see with new eyes both their humanity and God at work in their lives and yours.

Silent worship doesn't mean it all has to be inside, either. You can leaf through a Bible or other spiritual reading. You might want to pick up a hymnal and sing praises. Or not pick up a hymnal—just stand and sing from the heart. That's what happened at a New England Meeting that Benjamin Lloyd attended.

This past Fourth of July, a man stood and sang "America the Beautiful."

> . . . He sang it slowly. . . . It was not accomplished singing, but it was powerful ministry. . . . Great ministry travels on the wings of feeling, not in the nicely wrapped box of the Neat Idea.

That's one nice thing about Quaker worship—to paraphrase a famous chain restaurant's theme—"No rules, just right."

Welcome joy, especially the joy that comes from a powerful peace. This filling may make you want to smile. That's okay, too. It may lead you to speak—or may lead you into even deeper silence.

As you pass through the deep silence, you move into communion. No timer goes off. No bell rings. You'll know you are there, because you sense it's time to stop asking God to speak. You will know it is time for concentrated listening. It may help to imagine hearing God's voice. What would it sound like? In Peggy Payne's short story "The Pure in Heart," the Rev. Swain Hammond, pastor of a Presbyterian Church in Chapel Hill, North Carolina, hears the voice of God. "The voice is unmistakable. At the first intonation, the first rolling syllable, Swain wakes, feeling the murmuring life of each of a million cells." What would God sound like to you? How will you know God is speaking? Are you ready to hear God? Are you willing to share a spoken word from God to those who have gathered for worship?

This time of communal communion is a measure of our trust in God's presence and leading. It is just us—and God. This is trust. As John Bellows wrote, "I know of no other way, in these deeper depths, of trusting in the name of the Lord, and staying upon God, than sinking into silence and nothingness before Him. . . ."

In this sinking silent time, God comes and speaks to us. Again, what makes this possible is not the set time or place—it is our desire to meet God. This was true of the time Nancy and I went to Doc's Place, a nightclub. Our friends John and Vicki were celebrating their thirtieth wedding anniversary. He's a medical doctor, blues-rock musician, and owner of the nightclub. She teaches mediation and writes. They're engaged with peace and justice issues and practice their faith in the way they live—simply and carefully. They belong to the Friends church where I was the pastor.

They were married three decades ago in a mountain meadow above Boulder, Colorado, in a traditional Friends service. It was time to celebrate, and since John owns a nightspot, they invited everyone to "Doc's" for an evening of music and memories. Vicki's sisters' singing group performed, as did John's band, "The Walking Catfish." An eclectic mix, around 200 strong, gathered at the downtown nightspot. There were old people, kids, Quakers, rock musicians, social activists, university professors, a dyslexic carpenter, and many others. Some drank bottled water. Some drank soda pop. Some drank beer. The music played, people talked, the air was festive.

Then Vicki stepped on stage. That's when worship started. Vicki's a quiet person. Strong, but quiet—unlike her husband, who's a raconteur. She spoke into the microphone. The crowd quieted. She explained how she and John had married thirty years earlier and that they were going to renew their vows on stage that night. Then she went on to describe their wedding on the Colorado mountain. She told how traditional Quaker weddings are held in silence. How no minister is needed to officiate because God performs the wedding. How everyone who attends is a witness and signs the marriage certificate. But most of all, how this silence is set in worship. The couple listens for God. When the holy silence is deepest, they stand and recite their vows to each other.

"We're going to renew our vows," she said. "I'm going to say the same words I said to John thirty years ago. And after I say them, I'm going to say more about the thirty years we've had together." She paused. "And I am going to say them out of the silence," she continued, "when God tells me the time is right." John, standing beside her, nodded in agreement. "When Quakers gather in silence," she explained, "they do so expecting God to be present and bless them and speak to them in the silence. When we get quiet before God, as a group, we have what Quakers call a 'gathered meeting.' So let's get quiet before God now."

Then she and John sat down on two chairs placed on the stage. They bowed their heads in silence. Everyone there joined them. A holy hush filled that room. Not a Coke was slurped. Not a beer bottle clanked. Not a little baby cried. God's Holy Spirit wafted through that room and each heart. I looked around the room at the bowed heads—rockers, doctors, Quakers, movers and shakers. We all felt that we were in God's presence.

As I sat there, time moving slowly, yet too quickly, I remembered two Scriptures. One was Jesus' first miracle—turning water into wine. At a wedding. I couldn't help remembering that story as I sat at this wedding anniversary and beheld beer drinkers turned into silent worshipers. Another miracle wrought by Christ's Spirit moving among us.

Which brought the second verse to mind: "For where two or three come together in my name, there am I with them." Vicki brought us to a holy place when she explained Quaker worship and invited us into it. Jesus was with us. We fed on Him in our souls.

As the hour (or whatever time you've allotted) draws to an end, you'll want to close your silent worship by re-acknowledging God's blessings of warm wool socks, good friends, and peaceful hearts. This is the sending—preparing to reenter the world, better prepared, thanks to this rejuvenating time with God and each other, to live well in it. You'll be leaving as a renewed person, ready to witness with your life to the love and presence of God. You go out to, as Quakers say, let your life speak. With God going with and in you, your life will speak with fresh eloquence even in life's ordinary circumstances.

A typical way of ending is the handshake of peace. When worship is over, as sensed by the person who organized the service, he or she shakes hands with the person next to him. That handshake is then passed, as Christ's peace and benediction, around the room.

Quietude Query

�'ᔓ Relax your body and mind.

➭ Breathe deeply.

➭ Put down the book.

➭ Think about the following Quietude Query slowly and gently. Savor each thought.

⏋ Have I ever been a part of a "non-church" experience where I felt God's presence? What made me feel that God was there?

You've probably noticed that the above includes all of the elements of worship that you find in the traditional liturgies. There's the assembly of the people—Gathering and Welcoming; the service of the word—Deep Worship; the Eucharist—Communion; and the dismissal—the Sending Forth. But since there is no outward form, Quaker communal silence invites us to actively participate in the larger tradition that all Christians profess. Quaker silent worship brings us together as equal members of Christ's body. Noses, hands, feet . . . even armpits (though I doubt that Paul thought of them when writing that we are Christ's body) come with no hierarchy of age, wisdom, intellect, or experience. In communal silence, we find ourselves empowered to walk together a bit further down the pilgrim way.

CHAPTER SIX

A Holy Hush

Nancy and I settled into the silence of Plainfield Friends Meeting. Plainfield Friends in Indiana is 900 miles and a tradition away from South Starksboro Friends in Vermont. It's brick instead of clapboard and has all the modern conveniences—an elevator, heating and air conditioning, a sound system, and lots of paved parking. Where Quakers in South Starksboro meet in a traditional silent worship, these Indiana Quakers have followed the more than one hundred-year-old Midwestern practice of having a Friends pastor. To a non-Friend, the difference would be that one group has a pastor and the other doesn't. To a Quaker the difference is that South Starksboro is "unprogrammed" (no part of worship is programmed—the Spirit is free to move whenever) and Plainfield is "programmed" (the Spirit moves through the hymns, children's message, sermon, and silence). The point they share is their emphasis on silence.

While Plainfield Friends' bulletin may look similar to that of Plainfield United Methodist Church or Plainfield Christian Church, what goes on is different in tone and spirit. What's different is the holy silence. We have a long silence before the morning prayer and an even longer one after the sermon.

This morning we had a guest pastor. She did a wonderful job of helping us see how the story of the Good Samaritan applied to us. After she concluded the sermon, a holy hush fell over the room. It began in the front of the unadorned Meetingroom and rolled back through to the library, where the small overflow and latecomers (like Nancy and me) were sitting.

A young boy sat on the floor, coloring as the silence flowed over us. As I closed my eyes, I saw him look up at his grandfather and ask in a whisper, "Why's it so quiet?"

It's quiet because Jesus is here, I wanted to say. I didn't hear what his grandfather told him. It was enough for me to know that this boy had heard the silence—and recognized that it had a quality that set it apart. I looked over at Nancy. There was a smile on her face. She'd heard the boy's question. I knew her answer was the same as mine. I reached for her hand and settled more deeply into God's love.

Acknowledgments

Gratitude, like silence, is sometimes hard to form into words. One of the blessings in writing this book, for which I'm grateful, was the assistance of many good friends as I worked on *Holy Silence*. This includes Max Carter of Guilford College, Peggy Spohr, and Quaker pastors Josh Brown and Don Perry who, along with others, sent me suggestions for books to include in the "suggestions for reading" section. My colleagues at the Indianapolis Center for Congregations, especially Tim Shapiro, often dropped in with advice and encouragement.

Three other friends made special contributions to this project. David Lott agreed to turn his editorial eye to *Holy Silence*. As a fine Lutheran, David also added spiritual depth and understanding to the project. Added to this were injections of humor just when needed.

Susan Weber, a congregational consultant from Indianapolis, also read drafts of *Holy Silence*. Sue is a woman of deep personal faith. She frequently brings me good spiritual writing—like the poems and prayers in *God in Ordinary Time: Carmelite Reflections on Everyday Life*—at times when I especially need them. While I am a believer in the catholicity of the Church, it was also helpful to have a true Catholic read and comment on the book.

T. Canby Jones, my professor and mentor from Wilmington College, delighted me by agreeing to lend his vast Quaker experience and great heart to this project. Canby is a man of spiritual depth, discernment, and good humor. He continues to bless me.

Lil Copan, my editor at Paraclete Press, used a whip and dire threats to press me to write clearly and mindfully. Thanks, Lil.

Each of these good friends—Lil, David, Sue, and Canby—made this a better book than I could have done on my own. Of course, any mistakes in theology or clarity are mine, not theirs.

Finally, I am indebted to my wife, Nancy. A woman of uncommon grace and dignity (with just a touch of smart-aleckness), she remains my constant. Blessed with a spiritual center and a loving heart, she encouraged my writing and my silence. She always reminds me to think a little bit less and care a little bit more and communicate that caring in what I'm writing. For both her care and her thinking, I'm grateful.

Queries

FURTHER EXERCISES IN QUIETUDE

Since Quakers don't have a formal creed or a prayer book against which to measure faithfulness, we developed the concept of asking questions of ourselves, individually and corporately, as a gauge of faith and practice. This method began in the seventeenth century with the now quaint name of "Queries." Queries are sets of questions rooted in Quaker faith and life as informed by Friends' history, collective Quaker wisdom, and the Bible. The Queries are meant to be a form of guided self-examination, but they aren't meant to be an outward set of rules. In that sense, there are no outwardly defined correct answers. Rather, the Queries give us a framework within which we can look at and consider prayerfully the direction of our lives and the life of our worshiping community. As Baltimore Yearly

Meeting's *Faith and Practice* says, "Let each of us find a way into the silence which allows us to deepen our awareness of the divine and to find the inward source of our strength" (Advices and Queries, 1.02-3). You might find the following queries helpful as you develop your practice of holy silence. Use them the same way as the Quietude Queries sprinkled throughout the book—relax your body and mind, breathe deeply, put down the book, and think about the Query slowly and gently.

Individual Queries

➴ Do I try to set aside times of quiet for openness to the Holy Spirit?

➴ Do I encourage in myself a habit of relying on God's guidance for each day?

➴ Are my private holy silences a source of strength and guidance for daily living?

➴ In holy silence, do I respond to the leadings of the Holy Spirit, without trying to decide in advance what those leadings may be?

➴ Do I spend time daily in prayerful meditation, Bible reading, or other devotional activities that help put me in touch with my spiritual center?

➴ Am I open to the healing power of God's love?

↶ How does Jesus speak to me today?

↶ Am I aware of the Spirit of God at work in the ordinary activities and experiences of daily life?

↶ Am I open to new leadings from God?

↶ Have I approached this day's holy silence with a sense of quiet reverence?

↶ Am I ready to yield to God's will?

↶ Am I developing an attitude of expectant waiting?

↶ As my holy silence comes to a close, have I listened fully to all that has been spoken and unspoken?

↶ What can I take with me as I leave my silent time?

Communal Queries

↶ How do we prepare our hearts and minds for worship?

↶ Do our meetings give evidence that we come to them with hearts and minds prepared for communion with God?

🝰 Are our gatherings for silent communal worship held in a spirit of expectant waiting and communion with the Holy Spirit?

🝰 Are our gatherings for silent communal worship held in a spirit of expectant waiting for divine guidance?

🝰 How do we integrate what happens in our silent communal worship into our daily lives?

🝰 Do we seek opportunities for worship outside of communal silence?

🝰 How does the vocal ministry of the meeting contribute to our group's spiritual life?

🝰 Is there a living silence into which we feel drawn together by the presence of God?

🝰 Are we sensitive to one another's needs, and do we respond to the Spirit's promptings to minister, whether in silence or through the spoken word?

🝰 Are we in harmony with others in the room? Can we hear another's message even if it initially seems remote?

ANNOTATED NOTES

CHAPTER ONE

p. 3 ". . .where two or three come together in my name, there am I with them." Matthew 18:20.

p. 4 "The Word became flesh and made his dwelling among us. We have seen his glory, the glory of the One and Only, who came from the Father, full of grace and truth." John 1:14.

p. 6 "When Elijah heard it, he wrapped his face in his mantle and went out and stood at the entrance of the cave." 1 Kings 19:11-12 (NRSV)

p. 7 "Well, if it's a symbol, to hell with it." Paul Elie, Flannery O'Connor, quoted in *The Life You Save May Be Your Own: An American Pilgrimage* (New York: Farrar, Straus, and Giroux, 2003), 176.

p. 7-8 ". . . the very crown and culmination of what we can do with our human life here on earth." Rufus Jones, quoted in *Christian Faith and Practice in the Experience of the Society of Friends* (London: London Yearly Meeting of the Religious Society of Friends, 1960), #244.

p. 8 "Outwardly, all silences seem alike. . . ." Thomas Kelly, quoted in *Christian Faith and Practice in the Experience of the Society of Friends*, #245.

p. 8 "Be still and know that I am God." Psalm 46:10 (RSV)

CHAPTER TWO

p. 12 "What is Silence? It is the Great Mystery! The Holy Silence is His voice!" Kent Nerburn, ed., *The Soul of an Indian and Other Writings from Ohiyesa* (Novato, CA: New World Library, 2001), 10.

p. 12 "Those who know do not talk. Those who talk do not know." Tao Te Ching #56.

p. 12 ". . . and what is elusive and deceptive resolves itelf into crystal clearness." www.calnqm.org/Downingtown/Downingtown_2003_12.htm.

p. 13 " . . . just the right moment." Ecclesiasticus 20:7 (NJB)

p. 13 "Let all the earth keep silence before him." Habakkuk 2:20 (RSV)

p. 14 "Speak, Yahweh, for your servant is listening." 1 Samuel 3:9 (NJB)

p. 14-15 ". . . boat to a lonely place by themselves." Mark 6:30–32 (RSV)

p. 15 See Galatians 1:15–18.

p. 15-16 "Arsenius, flee, keep silence, and lead a life of silent contemplation, for these are the fundamental causes which prevent a man from committing sin." E. A.

W. Budge, ed. and trans., *The Paradise or Garden of the Holy Fathers*, 2 vols. (London: Chatto & Windus, 1907), vol. 2: 3. (Arsenius, who lived in the fifth century, was a member of a noble Roman family and a scholar of Greek literature and philosophy. He fled Constantinople and lived as a solitary for 59 years.)

p. 16 "Nothing in all creation is so like God as silence."
www.spiritualityhealth.com/newsh/items/bookreview/item_9348.html

p. 16-17 ". . . the mother of holy and lofty thoughts." Joseph Rickaby, trans., *The Practice of Perfection and Christian Virtues*, 3 vols. (Chicago: Loyola Univ. Press, 1929), vol. 2: 111, 120.

p. 18 "God can truly create an inner sanctuary in us." www.christianyoga.us/home.htm

p. 18-19 ". . . understanding the God in YOU." Elizabeth Baron, www.elizabethbaron.com/

p. 19 ". . . a method of preparing the soul for spiritual experiences" James Hasting, ed., *Encyclopedia of Religion and Ethics* (New York: Charles Scribner's Sons, 1908), s.v. "Silence."

p. 20 ". . . might come to receive freely from Him." Rufus Jones, ed., *George Fox: An Autobiography* (public domain) scanned and edited by Harry Plantinga, 61.

p. 20 ". . . the more suitable to the language of a spirit." William Penn, quoted in *Christian Faith and Practice in the Experience of the Society of Friends*, #227.

p. 21 "Christ has come to teach His people Himself." John N. Nickalls, ed., *Journal of George Fox* (London: London Yearly Meeting of the Religious Society of Friends, 1975), 98.

p. 22 ". . . I have made known to you." John 15:14-15 (RSV)

p. 23-24 "This openness and living experience is achieved through silence." Wilmer Cooper, *Friends and the Sacraments* (Richmond, IN: Friends United Press, 1981), 3.

p. 24 ". . . this is our Eucharist and our Communion." London Yearly Meeting, 1928, quoted in *Christian Faith and Practice in the Experience of the Society of Friends* #241.

p. 24-25 Steve Silson, "Worshiping Mr. Loh: Our personal deity is a 76-year-old Chinese guy." *The Utne Reader*, May/June 2004.

p. 26 ". . . answering that of God in everyone." John N. Nickalls, ed., *Journals of George Fox* (London: London Yearly Meeting of the Religious Society of Friends, 1975), 263.

p. 26 "Isn't this the carpenter?" Mark 6:3

p. 26 "And Jesus grew in wisdom and stature, and in favor with God and men." Luke 2:52

p. 28 ". . . though the guiding hand rested upon us so lightly that we were unaware of its touch." William Littleboy, quoted in *Christian Faith and Practice in the Experience of the Society of Friends* #82.

p. 29-30 "Holy as a Day is Spent." Carrie Newcomer, BMI, © 2002, Carrie Newcomer, BMI, administered by Bug Music. Used by permission of Carrie Newcomer.

p. 30 "We find Him when we enjoy beauty." Kerry Walters, *Rufus Jones: Essential Writings* (Orbis, 2001), 74.

p. 31 ". . . will sing for joy before the LORD." 1 Chronicles 16:33

p. 31 "For the LORD is good; his love endures forever." Psalm 100:4-5

p. 32 "that brazen expectation [of hearing the voice of God]." Scott Russell Sanders, *The Force of Spirit* (Boston, MA: Beacon Press, 2000), 155.

p. 32 "We know that we have a place in God's purpose." Ruth Fawell, quoted by Beatrice Saxon Snell in *A Joint and Visible Fellowship*, Pendle Hill Pamphlet #140 (Wallingford, PA: Pendle Hill, 1965), 10.

p. 33 ". . . gathered of the living God into a sense of the enjoyment of his divine and living presence." Thomas Story, quoted in *Christian Faith and Practice in the Experience of the Society of Friends*, #44.

p. 33-34 ". . . we lie down quietly in peace, for all is well." Thomas R. Kelly, *A Testament of Devotion* (New York: Harper & Brothers, 1941), 124.

CHAPTER THREE

p. 35 "True silence is the rest of the mind; and is to the spirit, what sleep is to the body, nourishment and refreshment." William Penn, quoted in *Quaker Faith and Practice: Second Edition* (London: The Yearly Meeting of the Religious Society of Friends ((Quakers)) in Britain), #20:11.

p. 35-36 "This was, therefore, the first house I was in, or slept in, in Philadelphia." Charles Van Doren, *Benjamin Franklin* (Garden City: Garden City Publishing, 1941), 40.

p. 36 "Come to me, all you who are weary and burdened, and I will give you rest." Matthew 11:28.

p. 37 ". . . all the resources of our almost miraculous technology have been thrown into the current assault against silence." Aldous Huxley, quoted by George H. Gorman in *The Amazing Fact of Quaker Worship* (London: Friends Home Service Committee; 1973), 20.

p. 44 "I think I'm an alright guy I know I ain't perfect but God know I try." "Alright Guy" by Todd Snider, 1994 Bro'N Sis Music, Inc./Keith Sykes Music (BMI) from the album "Songs for the Daily Planet" (MCA, 1994).

p. 46-47 "Its strength and vigor can be alarming when we meet it for the first time." David Runcorn, *The Center of Quiet* (Downer's Grove, IL: Intervarsity Press, 1990)

p. 47 "Its strength and vigor can be alarming when we meet it for the first time." David Runcorn, *The Center of Quiet* (Downer's Grove, IL: Intervarsity Press, 1990), 17.

p. 49 "You are my friends if you do what I command you." John 15:14 (RSV)

p. 49 "You have already been told what is right and what Yahweh wants of you. Only this, to love loyalty and to walk humbly with your God." Micah 6:8 (NJB).

p. 50 "He has showed you, O man, what is good. And what does the LORD require of you? To act justly and to love mercy and to walk humbly with your God." Micah 6:8 (RSV)

p. 50 "I have never repented of silence." E. A. Wallis Budge, *The Paradise of the Holy Fathers*, Vol. II, (Seattle: St. Nectoarios Press, 1984, 319-320). (Abba Arsenius was born in Rome circa 360. He was well educated, of senatorial rank, and served as a tutor to the sons of Emperor Theodosius I. At the age of thirty-four, Arsenius sailed secretly from Rome to Alexandria and from there to Scetis where he became a monk under Abba John the Dwarf. Abba Arsenius went to the Lord in 449.)

p. 50 See "The light shines in the darkness, and the darkness has not overcome it." John 1:4 (NRSV)

p. 50-51 ". . . and discerning the thoughts and intentions of the heart." Hebrews 4:12 (RSV)

p. 51-52 ". . . sucking up God's gift of life and being restored." Tayeko Yamanouchi, quoted *in Quaker Faith and Practice: Second Edition* (London: The Yearly Meeting of the Religious Society of Friends ((Quakers)) in Britain), #2:54.

p. 52 ". . . to allay all storms and tempests." George Fox, quoted at www.bible.org/illus/r/r-50.htm.

p. 52–54 "God Himself as my life and my all." Martin Hope Sutton, "Silence: # 553." Used by permission of the Tract Association of Friends, www.tractassociation.org/hitec.htm.

p. 54 ". . . free to take his kindled heart and go. . . ." From the privately published volume *The House at Rest* (1984) by Jessica Powers. From *The Selected Poetry of Jessica Powers*, published by ICS Publications, Washington, D.C. All copyrights, Carmelite Monastery, Pewaukee, WI. Used by permission. (Jessica Powers was a poet and Carmelite nun with the religious name of Sister Miriam. She died in 1988.)

p. 57 "Silence is best when the ways of the Lord are hidden from our eyes." Shlomo Du Nour, *Adiel* (New Milford, CT: The Toby Press, 2002), p. 93.

p. 57-58 ". . . and above all, letting ourselves be used in it." Diana Lampen, *Facing Death* (London: Quaker Home Service, 1979), 22, 27.

p. 58 ". . . we meet God, are empowered, and finally led to the service of others." Roger J. Vanden Busch "The Value of Silence in Quaker Spirituality," *Spirituality Today*, Winter 1985, Vol. 37, 326–335.

CHAPTER FOUR

p. 65 ". . . not to think of yourself more highly than you ought to think." Romans 12:3 (NRSV)

p. 66-67 "When evening came, he was there alone." Matthew 14:1–23

p. 67 "Very early in the morning, while it was still dark, Jesus got up, left the house and went off to a solitary place, where he prayed." Mark 1:35

p. 71 "We have all heard this holy Whisper at times." Thomas R. Kelly, *A Testament of Devotion*, 116.

p. 71-72 ". . . in the lowly Seed, of all that springs and arises in thy heart." Isaac Pennington, quoted by Roger J. Vanden Busch in "The Value of Silence in Quaker Spirituality," *Spirituality Today*, Winter 1985, Vol. 37, 326–335.

p. 73-74 "He expected this secret to be freshly discovered in everyone who would be His follower." Thomas R. Kelly, *A Testament of Devotion*, 32.

p. 77 "The word born of silence must be received in silence." Pierre Lacout, quoted in *Quaker Faith and Practice: Second Edition,* #2:12.

p. 77-78 " . . . with all the news/ I can bear." Sharron Singleton, "All the News," *Christian Century*. Reprinted with permission from the August 10, 2004, issue of *The Christian Century*, 8.

p. 78 "We find time for what we *really want* to do." Thomas R. Kelly, *A Testament of Devotion*, 120.

p. 80 "For God alone my soul waits in silence, for my hope is from him." Psalm 62:1,5 (RSV)

p. 81-82 "Praise to you again and again. Amen." John Fischer, "The Lord's Prayer" (words and music by John Fischer, © 1969 by F.E.L. Publications, Ltd. Used by permission of John Fischer.)

p. 82 " . . . until he learned to be silent." Thomas Merton, *The Wisdom of the Desert* (New York: New Directions, 1960), p. 30.

p. 82-83 ". . . our many failures." Thomas F. Green, quoted in *Christian Faith and Practice in the Experience of the Society of Friends*, #239.

p. 85 "The Savior is . . . IN." Tony Hendra, *Father Joe: The Man Who Saved My Soul* (New York: Random House, 2004), 230.

p. 87 "And hear the song of hope she sings." John Greenleaf Whitter, "Revelation," *Selections from the Religious Poems of John Greenleaf Whittier* (Philadelphia: The Tract Association of Friends, 1999), 54-55. (Whittier is largely ignored today, but his poetry was immensely popular in his time, especially his sentimental verse—"Snow Bound: A Winter Idyll" and "Barbara Frietchie": "'Shoot, if you must, this old gray head/but spare your country's flag,' she said." His spiritual sensibilities ran deep and he communicated them very well, which is why many of his religious poems still speak today. His "Dear Lord and Father of Mankind" is perhaps the best-known Quaker hymn.)

CHAPTER FIVE

p. 91 ". . . in worship there comes a spiritual harmony." London Yearly Meeting, quoted in *Christian Faith and Practice in the Experience of the Society of Friends*, #234.

p. 91 ". . . those who persevere in group worship know that it differs from private devotion as the music of an orchestra differs from the music of a single player." Beatrix Saxon Snell, *A Joint and Visible Worship* (Wallingford, Pennsylvania: Pendle Hill, 1965), 10.

p. 94 ". . . and that recognizes a direct one-to-one relationship with God." Robert Lawrence Smith, *A Quaker Book of Wisdom* (New York: Eagle Books, 1998), 10.

p. 95 "Everything you have asked for is granted." Rufus Jones, quoted by Marjorie E. Nelson in *Friends and Violence* (an on-line publication of Friends General Conference) www.fgcquaker.org/library/welcome/fa-violence.html

p. 101 ". . . some that seemed to me quite false, and I felt the need to answer them." John Omerod Greenwood, quoted in *Quaker Faith and Practice: Second Edition,* #2:68.

p. 102 "True godliness does not turn men out of the world, but enables them to live better in it and excites their endeavors to mend need it." William Penn, quoted in *Christian Faith and Practice in the Experience of the Society of Friends*, #395.

p. 102 ". . . indeed this is the surest way to become a Christian." Robert Barclay, quoted in *Christian Faith and Practice in the Experience of the Society of Friends,* #239.

p. 103 ". . . and to him who knocks it will be opened." Matthew 7:7-8 (RSV)

p. 108 "No moment of silence is a waste of time." Rachel Needham, quoted in *Quaker Faith and Practice: Second Edition*, #2:17.

p. 110 ". . . so the task is to cultivate a disposition of grateful receptivity." Michael Lawrence Birkel, *Silence and Witness: The Quaker Tradition* (Traditions of Christian Spirituality) (Maryknoll, NY: Orbis Books, 2004), 41.

p. 111 "In that also I saw the infinite love of God." John N. Nickalls, ed., *Journal of George Fox* (London: London Yearly Meeting of the Religious Society of Friends, 1975), 19.

p. 112 ". . . Great ministry travels on the wings of feeling, not in the nicely wrapped box of the Neat Idea." Benjamin Lloyd, "The Divine Source of Vocal Ministry," *Friends Journal,* December 4, 2004, 7.

p. 113 ". . . the murmuring life of each of a million cells." Peggy Payne, "The Pure in Heart," *God: Stories,* C. Michael Curtis, ed. (New York: Houghton Mifflin, 1998), 223.

p. 113 ". . . sinking into silence and nothingness before Him. . . ." John Bellows, quoted in *Quaker Faith and Practice: Second Edition*, #2:15.

p. 115-116 "For where two or three come together in my name, there I am with them." Matthew 18:20.

FriendsTalk

A GLOSSARY OF QUAKER WORDS
AND PHRASES

Quakers talk funny. Not with an accent or anything, except one that denotes what country or part of the United States they're from. They talk funny because, over their almost four-hundred-year history, they've developed a peculiar vocabulary. The following words and phrases are either in *Holy Silence* or are ones you might hear if you visit a Friends meeting.

As Way Opens: in accordance with specific promptings of the Holy Spirit as God's will becomes known. Taking one step at a time as it becomes clear what God wants you to do.

Centering Down: Concentrating on God and putting aside all other matters.

Children of Light: the first name used by George Fox's followers. By 1652 they were calling themselves "Friends."

Christ Within: the Spirit of Jesus in the soul, mind, and heart.

Communion: spiritual communication with God without ritual or outward symbols: inner listening for the Spirit of God.

Corporate Leading: divine guidance received by a group of worshipers.

Experiential: something which a man or woman has experienced and tested by living out.

Faith and Practice: a book published by a Yearly Meeting (the Quaker version of synod or diocese) that describes the beliefs of those Friends.

First Day: Sunday. Friends developed what they called "plain speech" and numbered the days and months rather than using names that come from non-Christian sources or are erroneous—for example, October is not the 8th (Oct) month, thus Friends called it Tenthmonth.

Friends: members of the Society of Friends. Also called Quakers.

Gathered Meeting: a worship group united in feeling the movement of the Spirit in and among them.

Good Raised Up: seeing evidence of good actions influenced by the Holy Spirit. The phrase comes from a quotation by Robert Barclay: "I found the evil weakening in me, and the good raised up."

Hold Silence: sitting in active, listening silence.

Inner Light: Jesus Christ as experienced inside us as we hold silence.

Leadings: direction or guidance coming from the Spirit of God.

Light (also Light Within): the presence of God or Christ in our souls. Other names are the Principle, the Seed, and the Truth.

Meeting: an appointed gathering of Friends. *Meeting* is used instead of church or congregation because of the expected participation of all in meeting God together.

Meeting for Worship: gathering to worship under the leading of the Spirit.

Meetingroom: the room where Meeting is held. Likewise, a meetinghouse is the building where Meeting is held. Meetinghouse is used, in established Friends organizations, instead of church.

Mind the Light: to follow the God's leading.

Moving: a compulsion to speak or act from a spiritual center as prompted by the Spirit.

Opening: a spiritual opportunity.

Programmed Meeting: a meeting for worship with pre-planned speaking and music. The majority of Friends congregations in the United States are either programmed or semi-programmed.

Quaker: nickname of Friend.

Quaker Grace: a time of silent prayer at the beginning of a meal.

Queries: questions for spiritual guidance to be asked and answered by individuals and worship groups. Each Faith and Practice contains a list of Queries.

Seekers: those searching for spiritual truth and God.

Speak to thy condition: a word or action that is particularly appropriate, helps clarify a situation, or settles and satisfies a soul's longing.

Unprogrammed Meeting: a "silent" Meeting with no paid pastor or order of worship. The traditional Friends way of worship, still practiced in many Meetings.

Words on Silence
SUGGESTIONS FOR READING

Quakers are writers. In fact, one our earliest nicknames was "Publishers of Truth." We are a small sect, with fewer than 200,000 members in the United States. Our influence in print, though, has far exceeded our numbers. Quakers have produced some of the most important literature of the last 350 years. Included among these are classics of devotional literature such as the journals of George Fox and John Woolman and works by William Penn, Thomas Kelly, and Richard Foster.

Quakers today write widely and thoughtfully in nonfiction and fiction (Haven Kimmel and Philip Gulley are two of the best known fiction writers). The list below features titles directly relating to Quaker silence and spirituality.

A Quaker Book of Wisdom: Life Lessons in Simplicity, Service, and Common Sense by Robert Lawrence Smith (Perennial: 1999). Smith, of Sidwell Friends School in Bethesda, Maryland, uses stories from his life to share the nature of the Quaker ideals of silence, worship, service, nonviolence, family, and more. It's a readable little book—and helpful, too.

A Testament of Devotion by Thomas R. Kelly (Harper SanFrancisco: 1996). This slender collection of five essays is a classic in contemporary Christian devotional literature (in print continuously since 1941). The depth of writing continues to fill readers with the desire to live close to God.

Encounter With Silence: Reflections from the Quaker Tradition by John Punshon (Friends United Press: 1987). English Quaker John Punshon's book is an in-depth look, theologically and spiritually, at the art and nature of Quaker worship. Its particular emphasis is on corporate worship.

Imagination & Spirit: A Contemporary Quaker Reader by J. Brent Bill (Friends United Press: 2003). This collection reflects some of the best Quaker non-fiction and fiction writing and features a brief biography of each author, including Thomas Kelly, Jessamyn West, James Michener, Daisy Newman, Jan de Hartog, and Scott Russell Sanders.

Journal and Major Essays of John Woolman by John Woolman, Phillips Moulton, ed. (Friends United Press: 1989). First published in 1774, Woolman's *Journal* is a devotional classic that focuses on spirituality and how it influences self, home, and community. Woolman was a leading anti-slavery activist of his time—well before the abolitionist movement or American independence. His writing is clear and beautifully moving.

Leadings: A Catholic's Journey Through Quakerism by Irene Lape (Brazos Press: 2002). This is the story of Lape's spiritual journey back to Catholicism—following a side-trip through Quakerism. A helpful little book about using various Christian traditions to find meaningful communion with God.

Prayer and Worship by Douglas V. Steere (Friends United Press: 1988). This is one of those Quaker devotional classics (first published in 1938) which encourages the reader toward a deeper spiritual life through prayer, worship, and devotional reading. Steere's writing renews our yearning for Divine encounters.

Quaker Spirituality: Selected Writings (Classics of Western Spirituality) by Douglas V. Steere (Paulist Press: 1984). Steere has assembled writings by the major voices of Quakerism from the seventeenth to the twentieth centuries, including George Fox, John Woolman, Isaac Penington, Thomas Kelly, Caroline Stephens, and Rufus Jones.

Rhythms of the Inner Life: Yearning for Closeness with God by Howard R. Macy (Barclay Press: 1992). Quaker Howard Macy uses the Psalms to explore longing, waiting, trembling, despairing, resting, conversing, and celebrating as ways to experience intimacy with God.

Rufus Jones: Essential Writings (Modern Spiritual Masters) by Rufus Matthew Jones, Kerry Walters (editor) (Orbis Books: 2001). Jones was a mystic, a social activist (he won a Nobel Prize as co-founder of the American Friends Service Committee), and a writer in the first half of the twentieth century. His writings focus on recognizing the presence of God in our lives, including our joys and sadnesses.

Silence and Witness: The Quaker Tradition (Traditions of Christian Spirituality) by Michael Lawrence Birkel (Orbis Books: 2004). Michael Birkel, who teaches at Earlham College in Richmond, Indiana, has written a delightful and insightful introduction to Quaker spirituality, including silent worship, prayer, discernment, and inner growth.

The Amazing Fact of Quaker Worship by George Humphrey Gorman (Friends Home Service Committee: 1973). This is a useful guide for anyone wanting to understand and experience Quaker worship.

The Eternal Promise: A Sequel to a Testament of Devotion by Thomas R. Kelly (Friends United Press: 1988). Though not nearly so well-known as *Testament of Devotion,* this collection, assembled after Kelly's death, contains some of his previously unpublished essays, including "Have You Ever Seen a Miracle?"

The Force of Spirit by Scott Russell Sanders (Beacon Press: 2001). A powerful book by a thoughtful, award-winning Quaker writer. In the best Quaker tradition, Sanders writes about spirituality in real life—in nursing homes, home building, and farmland, and in the silence of Quaker meeting.

The Quiet Eye: A Way of Looking at Pictures by Sylvia Judson (Regnery Publishing: 1982). Judson, a Quaker artist most famous (recently) for her sculpture "Bird Girl," featured in the book and movie "Midnight in the Garden of Good and Evil," gathered the pictures she used in her silence for this seventy-page book. She chose the ones she did, she says, because she wanted ". . . to find examples with a sense of 'divine ordinariness.'"

Many works of early Quakers dealing with the nature of holy silence are now available online at the Digital Quaker Collection of Earlham School of Religion (http://esr.earlham.edu/dqc/). Other digital resources can be found at www.quaker.org.

ABOUT PARACLETE PRESS

WHO WE ARE

Paraclete Press is an ecumenical publisher of books on Christian spirituality for people of all denominations and backgrounds.

We publish books that represent the wide spectrum of Christian belief and practice—from Catholic to Evangelical to liturgical to Orthodox.

We market our books primarily through booksellers; we are what is called a "trade" publisher, which means that we like it best when readers buy our books from booksellers, our partners in successfully reaching as wide an audience as possible.

We are uniquely positioned in the marketplace, without connection to a large corporation or conglomerate, and with informal relationships to many branches and denominations of faith, rather than a formal relationship to any single one. We focus on publishing a diversity of thoughts and perspectives—the fruit of our diversity as a company.

WHAT WE ARE DOING

Paraclete Press is publishing books that show the diversity and depth of what it means to be Christian. We publish books that reflect the Christian experience across many cultures, time periods, and houses of worship.

We publish books about spiritual practice, history, ideas, customs and rituals, and books that nourish the vibrant life of the church.

We have several different series of books within Paraclete Press, including the bestselling Living Library series of modernized classic texts, A Voice from the Monastery—giving voice to men and women monastics on what it means to live a spiritual life today, and Many Mansions—for exploring the riches of the world's religious traditions and discovering how other faiths inform Christian thought and practice.

Learn more about us
at our website: www.paracletepress.com,
or call us toll-free at (800) 451-5006.